CLIMATE CHAMPIONS

15

WOMEN FIGHTING FOR YOUR FUTURE

RACHEL SARAH

CHICAGO
REVIEW
PRESS

Published by Chicago Review Press Incorporated
814 North Franklin Street
Chicago, Illinois 60610
ISBN 978-1-64160-700-1

Library of Congress Control Number: 2022948972

Cover design and illustrations: Sadie Teper
Interior design: Nord Compo

Printed in the United States of America
5 4 3 2 1

There must be those
among whom we can sit
down and weep and still
be counted as warriors.

—Adrienne Rich

For girls and women everywhere . . .
especially my two hearts: Mae and Camille

Contents

Introduction

The night is dark, and my daughters are in bed. I'm transcribing another interview at my desk when my phone flashes with a "red flag" warning. In the San Francisco Bay Area, where we live, there's a dry lightning threat with strong wind gusts. It's not a good combination.

We haven't had any rain here for months. The hills are so dry that a spark could send them up in flames. I shut my eyes and try to breathe. Firefighters up north are still battling California's two biggest wildfires (Dixie and Caldor). A lightning storm would be devastating.

I return to my notes, trying to contain my despair. There's a note tacked above my desk that says, "Decide to hope."

But often it feels like hope itself is a scarce resource to draw on.

To write this book, I reached out to women around the world who are tirelessly working to repair our climate. They are scientists, policymakers, journalists, lawyers, activists, professors, researchers, and organizers.

They have, among other things:

- protected marine life and animals
- slowed down global warming and rising sea levels
- worked to sustain coastlines, forests, and ecosystems
- produced podcasts about climate cases around the world
- inspired students to learn about biology, ecology, and the climate
- driven national climate action plans
- testified to the leaders of their countries to protect, restore, and sustain land and water
- educated people about sustainable solutions and pushed polluters to pay
- founded organizations like Black Girl Environmentalist and Black Marine Science

Their lives are absorbed in seeking solutions. They've persevered harder than ever through the COVID-19 pandemic. And yet they said yes to talking to me.

In 2015 world leaders signed the Paris Agreement, which committed them to keep the planet from warming more than 1.5 or 2 degrees Celsius. Scientists agree that even 1.5 degrees of warming will have a significant impact on the planet, so consider how much worse it will be if we continue emitting heat-trapping gases unchecked.

As atmospheric scientist Katharine Hayhoe says, "Right now, Earth is running a fever and that fever affects everything we care about—our food, water, health, safety, economy, national security, and even our recreational activities."

These climate leaders rallied me: **It's not too late to act.**

In this book, they walk you through the steps to change. They show us what we can—and must—do for our future. Saving the world is overwhelming, and these women reminded me that the world is right outside our windows. They are facing the most pressing challenges we've ever experienced, rather than turning away.

Their advice? Do the work. Join an organization. Be brave. Ask for help. Imagine a new world. And most important, get into nature.

One night while I was transcribing an interview, I heard a sound outside. *Hoot hoot.* A great horned owl was calling out from one of the trees behind my home. The next night, there it was again. And again. This owl has been serenading the neighborhood every night as I've been writing.

These women have reminded me to support the people who are on the front lines. They've encouraged me to look at the trees outside my window, to take a walk around my neighborhood and to connect to people.

I hope that you, too, will see how they are standing up for all of us, and why the world needs more women making decisions. My gratitude for their time and dedication is as wide as the ocean.

Part I
Challenge the System

1

Molly Kawahata:
Keep on Climbing

Molly Kawahata is scaling her first-ever peak in Yosemite, pulling herself up a freezing wall of ice in the darkness to get to the top as she grips the next crag to ascend another inch.

"I'm *not* a morning person," Molly laughs. "But climbers climb early, so I guess I'm an aspiring morning person."

It's challenging to get up at 2 AM, but it's worth it to Molly. "There's something amazing about waking up in the middle of the night and being on the mountain when the sun is rising. It's magical to be on the glacier in the darkness. It's also safer to climb when everything is frozen and the mountain is more glued together."

Molly makes her way up to the top of the mountain with a headlamp shining and a trustworthy climbing partner on the other end of the rope. Patience, power, and persistence. These are her superpowers.

Molly was born and raised in Palo Alto in the San Francisco Bay Area to a Japanese American father and Italian American mother who met at a lab where they were both working. She's close to her parents and talks to them often; they've gone through a lot together.

"When I was a teenager, I started experiencing anxiety and got misdiagnosed with depression," Molly says.

It turns out that she was living with bipolar II disorder. "I lived with an untreated mental illness for 10 years," she says. "The suffering was more than I could handle sometimes."

During this dark time, Molly felt pulled to get outside in nature. "I was not outdoorsy at all, but my mind just went there," she says. "I was super lucky to live near natural space, which a lot of people don't have."

"I'd never hiked before. I didn't even know what a trailhead—the point that marks the start of the trail—was," she laughs. "I googled it, but I still couldn't find an answer! That's how little experience I had." Still, she managed to locate a trailhead near her home, and she took off up the hill. "I took these long hikes on my own and discovered the refuge of the outdoors.

Getting the right treatment for her bipolar disorder started to alleviate Molly's episodes. "I was so grateful to get treated because the suffering could be intolerable," she says. "But at the same time, there was something lost in no longer getting to experience the extremes in which I lived all the time."

Hiking became a big part of her self-care. At one point Molly remembers thinking, *Hey, instead of hiking around the mountain, why can't I go up it?*

This is how Molly got interested in mountaineering and alpine climbing. "As a kid, I'd seen photos of alpinists climbing, and the landscape was so beautiful." *Alpine* means anything above the tree line—where trees can no longer grow because it's too cold or there's not enough oxygen. Alpine areas are often wide-open glaciated spaces that can resemble a moonscape. Climbing in these environments might take you to high altitude in a very remote place, with ice and snow on the mountain, and steep faces you climb to get to the top.

When Barack Obama was first running for president of the United States, Molly joined a group in high school called Students for Barack Obama, and by the time she graduated she was the organization's national high school director. Molly knew that young people were the key to electing Obama, so after school every day, she worked with a team of other students to map out strategies for student organizing. She even had the chance to introduce Obama at a rally in San Francisco!

Then Molly got accepted to University of California, Berkeley. She moved into her dorm to start her freshman year but ended up missing the first few days of school to catch a flight to Denver, Colorado, where she'd been elected to be a delegate at the 2008 Democratic National Convention. That year, Obama became the 44th president of the United States.

Not long after earning her bachelor's degree in psychology, Molly joined the Obama administration as a political appointee and went on to become a policy adviser for energy and climate change at the White House. She was only in her early 20s when she worked on a team responsible for implementing President Obama's energy policy agenda and Climate Action Plan to reduce carbon dioxide emissions.

Molly spent four years working at the White House, a time she describes as "historic" as her team pushed groundbreaking climate action forward. "Our focus was on systemic change—changing the very system causing climate change. We've spent too much time talking about arctic polar bears and melting glaciers," Molly says. "The average person struggling to get by doesn't have the luxury of being able to worry about things happening thousands of miles away. That's why we must solve climate change for everyone."

Molly points out that communities of color are significantly more likely to have to live near fossil fuel–burning power plants, toxic waste sites, and polluting highways. And because of it, frontline communities often have some of the highest childhood asthma rates in the country. They also have higher risk of heart disease, lung disease, cancer, and premature death. All because of pollution.

"We need to prioritize effective climate strategies," Molly adds. "We're only going to solve this crisis through systemic change. That means focusing on policy and campaigns."

Systemic Change, Not Climate Change

In 2018, then-15-year-old Swedish climate activist Greta Thunberg told world leaders: "If solutions within this system are so difficult to find, then maybe we should change the system itself."

What is systemic change? It's a big phrase to digest. When you have a system for doing something, it means that you have a certain method.

Like cleaning your room. Maybe you pick up all your clothes first and then you fold them. Then you dust the surfaces, vacuum, and mop. In other words, you have to be organized.

In the Western world, we've had a system in place for the ways we do things. Like how we supply power to our homes and buildings.

But what if our method is not working anymore? What if our current system is harmful? If we continue with the same plan, we're headed toward an existential threat to our civilization.

So . . . systemic change means that we need to radically change the way we think and act.

On Molly's last day at the White House, she says that President Obama asked her what she was going to do next. "I sort of misunderstood the question, thinking he meant in the immediate term," she says. "I was really burnt out, and all I could think about was taking a break. I told him I was going to climb in Alaska! Like a reflex, he looked me straight in the eye, smiled, and responded with 'and . . . ?'" she says.

"I didn't understand what he meant, and I stared dumbly at him while standing awkwardly in the Oval Office. . . . Until I realized he was asking what I was going to do with my life. I explained that climate change had become my life's work, and I planned to continue working on it. 'Great,' he responded with a smile, 'we expect you back in this fight.'"

In 2020 Molly was determined to get Democratic former vice president Joe Biden and US senator Kamala Harris into office. She started to think about new methods of campaigning—given that a lot of traditional ways of reaching voters weren't as effective at reaching younger generations. Using new platforms, such as dating apps, social media, or gaming platforms, could be the key to reaching young people where they are.

Molly organized a team that created training resources and spread the message of how to campaign to young voters in new ways, and it took off on social media. She says that her intention was to connect with people and tap into their experiences. "It's about telling your story, having authentic conversations, and explaining your own personal stake in this."

Today, Molly spends time in Bozeman, Montana, because "it has some of the best ice climbing in North America. As soon as I came here, I was totally entranced. There's a vibrant climbing community here."

She can climb frozen waterfalls in a magical canyon called Hyalite: "The canyon gets cold enough for the vertical water to freeze, and we use special equipment to climb them. Everyone's out having fun."

Every chance she gets, Molly speaks to people about climate action. She's often asked to speak on panels and podcasts. "There's a story about the climate crisis you're not being told," she says. "It's that this crisis is *solvable*. There's a zero-carbon promised land out there, and we are steadily marching toward it. But it will require all of us fighting for systemic change. Everyone has a role to play, and all are welcome in the climate movement."

Climbing could be a metaphor for the highs and lows that Molly feels many days. "For a long time, I thought happiness was really straightforward. I thought the intention was to avoid suffering. But it wasn't until I turned 30 that I realized that sadness and suffering in your life is inextricably linked to happiness and joy. You can't have one without the other. And there's something kind of beautiful in that."

Molly still slips into a dark place sometimes, but over the years she has gotten the help and developed the tools she needs to return to the light. "When you're down there in the darkness, just feeling around, you can't see anything. Sometimes the darkest and scariest parts of ourselves, deep below the surface, can haunt and control us without our knowledge from below. It can feel very threatening to let those feelings rise to the surface, but what I've learned in my life is that when you confront your demons, they actually dry up into thin air. Facing your insecurities, fears, and anxieties is incredibly empowering. When you confront them, they no longer control you."

The Scale of Hope

In 2022, Patagonia released *The Scale of Hope*, a film that follows Molly Kawahata's years in Obama's office, her love of alpine climbing, her family's story of internment during WWII, and her mental health struggles. Most of all, this movie shares Molly's positive vision of how we can respond to the climate crisis.

The film is free on YouTube, and the author (that's me, Rachel Sarah!) appears in the film when she interviews Molly for this book.

On a recent morning, Molly got up in the dark, turned on her headlamp, and packed for the day's climb. "There's something really magical about going up the glacier of a mountain," she says. "When something goes wrong, you have to keep going."

Molly explains what she means: "We tend to think that over time, things just get better. More human rights, more equality, more justice. What we're not always considering is the parallel world we'd be living in had people not fought for the rest of us. We assume progress would've come along anyway. How? Somehow. But make no mistake—change is not predestined. Progress happens not because of the natural force of the world, but in spite of it. That's what makes it so worthy of our work."

The purpose of the climate movement is to improve everybody's quality of life, Molly says. "We're fighting to make things better for everyone. To give everybody access to clean energy. To give more people access to the climate movement, and to make the climate movement fight for everybody."

Molly adds, "Solving the climate crisis is about creating opportunity. There's a promised land, and we are well on our way."

Follow Molly Kawahata Online

Website: https://www.systemicstrategies.com

Instagram: @mollykawahata

The Scale of Hope **film:** https://www.youtube.com/watch?v=BrmKoU2Oe5I

Trailblazer: Caroline Gleich

Caroline Gleich is a professional climber, athlete, and environmental activist. She's also one of Molly's good friends.

"I got to meet Molly on a trip to Washington, DC, with Protect Our Winters and we instantly bonded," Caroline says, referring to a Colorado-based organization of passionate outdoor people who campaign to protect the places they live and love from climate change.

"We instantly connected. I was grieving the recent loss of a best friend to an avalanche accident, Liz Daley." Liz had guided and taught Molly about mountaineering on a trip to climb Mt. Baker. "In the first hour we met, we were sharing tears and deep belly laughs."

Caroline learned to ski when she was only two years old. When she started going to school, there was a very strict dress code. "I grew up in Minnesota, which is known for having brutally cold winters," Caroline says. "The girls' uniform required us to wear skirts. I walked to school, and even with thick leggings, there were days I felt like my legs were going to freeze."

This was a turning moment for Caroline. "My mom sat me down and helped me write a petition, and then we collected signatures," she says. "A few years later, they changed the rules so girls could wear pants or skirts, any time of the year."

This experience is what turned Caroline into an activist.

When she was in high school, her family moved to Utah, and this is when she really took to the slopes. But she also experienced tragedy and loss. "When I was 15, I lost my half-brother to an avalanche," Caroline says. "Since then, I've lost over a dozen more friends to avalanches." Losing so many people she loved has made Caroline grateful for the friends and experiences she has had in her life.

Caroline went to the University of Utah, where she got a degree in anthropology. One of her requirements was an American national government class: "I had a professor who was smart, animated, and had a passion for teaching. He made his tests very difficult but would let students get as much extra credit as they wanted by attending forums and asking questions. He asked us, 'How do you want to engage with the government? Do you want your only interactions to be when you pay a speeding ticket or taxes, or do you want to actively come to the table to use the government as a solution to problem solving?' A lightbulb went off in my head, and I realized I could help change and improve the societal systems with activism by merging the skills my mom taught me with the inspiration from my professor."

In 2017 Caroline became the first woman in history to ski all 90 lines of the Chuting Gallery, a series of ski slopes in Utah's Wasatch Mountains. One of these chutes was where she'd lost her brother.

Caroline regularly testifies in front of Congress to protect public lands and water.

For example, in 2020 she testified to the House Committee on Natural Resources on the American Public Lands and Waters Climate Solution Act, a bill that would require us to achieve net-zero greenhouse gas emissions from public lands and waters by 2040.

"Public lands can and should be part of climate solutions, and I hope Congress takes action on this bill," she says.

"When I'm climbing up a mountain to ski down, I feel like I'm doing exactly what I was meant to do," Caroline adds. "I feel the same way when I testify to Congress, speak at a public hearing, or run an ultramarathon. They all involve big adrenaline rushes and take all my skills and focus to achieve. Those are my career highlights—all the projects I've done that take all my focus and energy to achieve."

Follow Caroline Gleich Online

Website: https://www.carolinegleich.com

Instagram: https://www.instagram.com/carolinegleich/

Trailblazer: Ashima Shiraishi

Rock climber Ashima Shiraishi, 20, is "a prodigy among prodigies," according to *GQ*, which calls her "an outlier in the climbing world, which was, and still is, overwhelmingly made up of well-off white people."

"When people find out that I climb, they're surprised because I'm so small," she says in a TedX talk she gave at age 13, describing how she's been climbing since she was six years old at Central Park in New York City.

Ashima was profiled in the *New Yorker* when she was a freshman in high school, when the magazine referred to her "possibly the best female rock climber ever."

She trains at indoor gyms in New York City and travels around the world to find the most difficult climbs. She's also vegan and the author of a picture book that came out in 2020, *How to Solve a Problem: The Rise (and Falls) of a Rock-Climbing Champion.*

Amy Westervelt:
Calling Out the System
One Podcast at a Time

It's late summer 2021, and a ring of fire surrounds Amy
Westervelt's town in Northern California, moving closer and
closer to her home just outside Tahoe National Forest. She has
already packed bags for her two sons and backed up the audio
files on her laptop in case she and her family have to evacuate.

"I can count on one hand the number of days we've been
able to be outside since June," Amy says about her life in
Lake Tahoe with two young children. That's a few days in
three months.

Firefighters have been battling this latest fire for weeks, so
Amy keeps her kids indoors all day with air purifiers running.
It's unsafe to breathe the smoky air. On top of the wildfires

raging, schools in California closed their doors a year prior because of the COVID-19 pandemic, so Amy is juggling work deadlines with homeschooling, too.

Fire season in California has been devastating for years, but global warming has intensified the scale and destruction over the past decade. In 2020, for example, the massive August Complex became the largest fire in the state's history.

Amy grew up in the '80s in California and remembers the long droughts and the phrase "global warming." But climate change "still seemed pretty abstract and far away until I was in my 20s," she says. "Today, I don't know any kid who was born in the last 20 years who ever had that moment of *not* knowing exactly what it was."

Today, as a climate journalist, Amy takes the most abstract stories and clarifies them. A fact finder at heart, she throws light on some of the loftiest, most elusive concepts in climate today.

Amy has overcome so many challenges in her life. When she and her twin brother were seniors in high school, Amy applied to college, while her brother begged their parents to sign forms for him to enlist in the US Marine Corps. "He convinced my mom to sign the papers to allow early enlistment at seventeen, and off he went to boot camp while I packed up a U-Haul and headed to Berkeley."

Amy landed at the University of California, Berkeley, and majored in comparative literature. A year into Marine Corps service, "My brother was found badly beaten on his base,"

Amy writes. "He had been stabbed fourteen times, had his head bashed in by some sort of blunt object, and had been pushed out a second-story window."

Amy says that she'll probably never know exactly what happened that day, but at age 18, he became a quadriplegic. "Now his VA benefits barely cover the cost of living."

Amy's first job was writing about shopping online for Shop Online 123, a shopping companion to *Better Homes & Gardens*. The site never saw the light of day.

She says that she wanted to become a journalist so she could keep learning new things and talking to interesting people. She covered every beat, from business and finances to travel and the environment. She has written for the *New York Times*, the *Washington Post*, *Rolling Stone*, the *Guardian*, the *Nation*, and more. She won the Edward R. Murrow Award for her exposé on the hidden environmental and human costs of Tesla's Gigafactory in Nevada. She also won the Rachel Carson Award for "women greening journalism."

After a decade of reporting for print, Amy decided that she wanted to learn something new: broadcast radio. So she contacted her local NPR member station in Reno, Nevada, and asked if she could be an "over-aged intern" for them. They taught her the ropes for a month or two "and then hired me as a staff reporter."

Then Amy and one of her colleagues decided to start a podcast, and she fell hard in love with podcasting. She's persistent about finding the truth, and she'll go great lengths to unearth evidence. For example, she researched oil companies all the way back to the 1960s and uncovered that oil executives—and even US government officials—knew how fossil fuels would exacerbate global warming.

These interviews became the foundation of Amy's award-winning, true crime–style podcast called *Drilled*. Amy knew that she was pitching something different that audiences hadn't heard before: a climate story line that tells stories about people and their struggles, instead of a data-based, scientific show.

Networks turned her down. "I pitched *Drilled* to other podcast companies, and they all said there was no audience for a narrative climate podcast. . . . And I really was just convinced they were all wrong."

Amy decided to create her own women-run podcast network—called Critical Frequency—to report, host, and produce *Drilled*. *Drilled* won the Online News Association Award for Excellence in Audio Digital Storytelling in 2019 and was named Best Green Podcast in the *iHeartRadio Podcast Awards* in 2020. (Critical Frequency also distributed the podcast *No Place like Home*, with Anna Jane Joyner, who's also featured in this book.)

Today, in addition to the award-winning podcast *Drilled*, Amy runs a companion website called Drilled News (part of Covering Climate Now), to report climate news from national and local outlets. And Critical Frequency has produced

16 shows, including half a dozen climate shows. It focuses on reported, narrative shows, still has an all-women team, and has produced award-winning shows for other companies too, including *This Land* for Crooked Media and *Unfinished: Short Creek* for Stitcher.

Hot Take

Critical Frequency bills its podcast *Hot Take* thus: "If you're looking for a climate show where people talk like humans, process real emotions, have an honest conversation about how climate change intersects with race, class, gender and literally everything—and who's really to blame . . . complete with air horns . . . Hot Take is for you!"

Amy started the podcast *Hot Take* with climate essayist Mary Annaïse Heglar. Mary's work opened people's eyes in the climate movement because it underscores climate change as a justice issue that intersects with every other justice issue.

As one of the few Black women to become a public figure in the climate space, Mary makes it clear that she's "more interested in being Black people's climate friend than the climate movement's Black friend, and she's very intentional about writing for and appearing in outlets that reach beyond the climate choir."

Mary also coined the term *greentrolling* and is known for cyberbullying fossil fuel companies on Twitter.

Amy and Mary sum up *Hot Take*: "We take a feminist, race-forward lens to the biggest story of our time. Some people might call it intersectional; we call it honest."

In the first season of *Drilled*, called The Origins of Climate Denial, Amy goes back to the 1970s and 1980s, when oil companies did cutting-edge research on climate change behind the scenes. But in the 1990s everything changed, and oil executives began funding campaigns to deny climate change. After reading the excellent reporting Inside Climate News, Columbia Journalism School, and the *Los Angeles Times* had done for their What Exxon Knew About Climate Change series, Amy felt like more people should be talking about this story and that maybe in podcast form it could reach more people. She also thought there was more to the story than what had previously been reported.

Amy spent months traveling to interview former Exxon employees and researching primary source documents that show how this company had been collecting data decades ago about climate change. For example, Amy came across a list of patents from oil companies dating back to the 1970s showing that they'd applied for machinery and boats to drill into the Arctic as it melted owing to warming temperatures.

"I wasn't sightseeing. I was scientist-seeing," Amy says about her in-depth interviews and research. By recording interviews with these Exxon employees, Amy could hear how the tone of their voices changed when she asked specific questions about climate studies. "None of it hits quite the same way in print," she says.

"I started thinking, *Climate denial?*" Amy says. "Pretty dumb tactic. Not genius. Why did it work so well? It's an appealing message to tell people that nothing needs to change. But is there more to it than that?"

That question prompted several more months of investigation and another *Drilled* season, The Mad Men of Climate Denial, looking at the century-long propaganda efforts of the fossil fuel industry before climate change appeared on the scene.

Amy has been covering climate for more than two decades now as an investigative journalist. She's highly respected by fellow journalists, who say that she "has transformed climate journalism."

"I've had a lot of people recently say stuff like, 'Amy, you just came out of nowhere and are everywhere on climate now,'" she says. "That's . . . not what happened." For the first decade of her career, she adds that she "waffled between optimism about tech solutions and depression about the state of things."

Then she got angry. Especially about climate disinformation. For more than a century, public relations firms have deflected responsibility and deceived the public to believe that we, as individuals, are to blame for environmental problems, including the climate crisis. "Climate disinfo" is what Amy calls it.

The climate crisis is a collective problem, Amy says. As individual people, we can't be responsible to solve problems alone.

"For too long, Americans were fed a false narrative that they should feel individually guilty about the climate crisis," Amy cowrites with Georgia Wright and Liat Olenick in a feature titled The Dirty Dozen: Meet America's Top Climate Villains, in which they profile the 12 American men—who are all White—who've "helped the fossil fuel industry destroy our planet."

"The reality is that only a handful of powerful individuals bear the personal responsibility," Amy, Georgia, and Liat write. "Working- and middle-class people must stop blaming themselves for the climate crisis. Instead, it's time to band together to seek justice and hold these profiteers accountable. Only in calling out their power and culpability is it possible to reclaim the world that belongs to all of us, together."

The need to organize collectively if we're going to change is a recurring theme in Amy's work. We're all in this together. This is what inspired Amy to write a book called *Forget "Having It All": How America Messed Up Motherhood—and How to Fix It* (Seal Press, 2018).

In an approach that's very characteristic to her, Amy researched the roots of mothers and motherhood dating back to the days when the colonists seized America and up to today. Amy asks deep questions about how much mothers do and how little they're compensated. (Because she was under pressure to keep working while mothering, two hours after giving birth to her younger son, Amy filed another story and then got straight back to her full-time job the next morning.)

"A lot of people maybe don't live near extended family or just don't have that kind of relationship with their family, but you can kind of create these bonds with people in your community," Amy says. "For example, I have a couple of my kids' friends whose parents and I trade off picking the kids up, and sometimes we'll trade off doing dinners at someone's house or whatever. Just find ways to kind of create that support system in your own life if it's not being offered to you externally."

Amy says that "the best solution to the climate crisis is community building."

"As someone who writes about rich dudes a lot, I often get asked, 'What can I do?' or 'What keeps you going?' And this is my answer: community. Community building, community organizing, community resilience, all of it."

In 2020, just before COVID-19 spread to the United States, her father took his own life. She describes hunting for her dad's suicide note in his car and never finding it. "In a few months we'd be quarantined, and the entire state of California would be on fire, but for now I was just sleepwalking through personal tragedy."

When it was safe to travel again, Amy made her way to Southern California to bury her father. She says that her dad was a man, like many of us, who believed he could solve all his problems on his own. He didn't realize that we're all in this together, that we can't resolve everything alone.

Amy was juggling so much, often on her own. After getting laid off in the early days of the pandemic, her husband had accepted a new job that took him on the road during the week, so he was only home on weekends. This meant that in addition to reporting and producing podcasts every day, Amy took care of her kids, ages five and nine. "I'd wake up at 2 AM to work, and then at 9 AM I'd launch into homeschooling."

When Amy's birthday rolled around, her husband offered to send her away on a solo trip so she could have some time alone. "My husband said, 'I'll send you away someplace to chill out,'" she says. "But I told him that I wanted to go and check out some archives," she laughs. "Yes, I wanted to spend it alone digging through archives."

So Amy spent her birthday doing what she loves: mining through files for a project in the works. She spent a week researching archives in Washington, DC, and the Midwest because at the end of the day, she is a truth seeker. "The thing I enjoy the most is sitting in the corner and reading documents," Amy says. "I'm a huge nerd for documents!"

Amy loves libraries. And research. "I'm a lifelong do-the-homework kind of person, and I don't say anything unless I've really locked down the receipts," Amy says.

Amy works with a lot of primary sources, which means documents, images, or artifacts that give you firsthand evidence about a topic, such as letters or a diary entry.

Amy also goes back decades to unearth information. "The reason denial and disinformation have worked so well is that the fossil fuel industry did a very good job of limiting how we think about environmental issues," Amy explains.

All through the pandemic, Amy did her best to balance work and family. She ploughed through work deadlines and scrambled to find childcare so she could set up interviews for a new climate podcast.

"Maybe these things sound completely unrelated—climate change, mental health care, childcare—but to me they are all layers to the same uniquely American issue: the idea that each of us can and should solve systemic problems on our own."

She continually asks people to understand the root causes of our problems, instead of hurrying to find the solutions. She also worries a lot about what the future will be like for not only her own kids but kids everywhere. "It fills me with both grief and white-hot rage," she writes in her essay "Mothering in the Age of Extinction." "Parents have always worried about their kids' futures and presents at the same time, and that goes double for mothers who are marginalized in any additional way."

Back to summer 2021, *Drilled* is now in its sixth season! In a miniseries in 2021 that Amy produced with climate reporter Dharna Noor, they took a deep look into *The ABCs of Big Oil*, or how oil companies "got into the education game, and why it worked so well."

"For decades, the fossil fuel industry has been distributing propaganda to limit how Americans think about taking on the climate crisis," Amy and Dharna say. "They haven't just done so through political lobbying and advertising. They've also taken a much more insidious route: shaping schools' curricula."

They wanted to know: How much corporate-sponsored content shows up in elementary, high school, and university curricula around the United States? And how does the fossil fuel industry's efforts shape the way that teens are thinking about economics, policy, and the climate?

Amy and Dharna took a close look at the STEM portal that Discovery Education promotes to high school guidance counselors and teachers. First, they found some great resources that are "particularly encouraging women in STEM and people of color."

But when they jumped over to the partner page for the STEM Careers Coalition, they found out that these programs are funded by oil and gas companies like Chevron and the American Petroleum Institute.

"It's like backdoor propaganda," they say, explaining this is how fossil fuel companies continue to infiltrate schools, "limiting how Americans are allowed to think about the environment and the economy."

Digging even deeper into the content partners, Amy and Dharna found out that many of these educational initiatives are connected to Lyda Hill Philanthropies, an organization founded by an oil heiress in Dallas, Texas, who is the grand-daughter of an oilman named H. L. Hunt.

In the fall, the wildfires have been raging closer to her home. Evacuation is impending. Somehow, Amy shows up to her kindergartner's orientation and then runs out to buy extra dog food while arranging for the release of a new podcast she produced.

"This is the second time in the last three years that we've left home because of a fire. Both times, I've tried to make it an adventure, a choice. I don't know if that's the right call or not, and frankly, I did it for me as much as them. I'm still not quite ready to accept what the rest of their lives will look like."

Amy hopes that maybe this crisis will finally wake up America. It's time that we realize how our systems are failing us. "It's the power structure, not the energy source," she likes to say.

Amy is incredibly resilient. She laughs, explaining that growing up, she felt like her mother didn't like her very much, so maybe she learned early on *not* to really care what people think about her. "If your mom doesn't like you, who cares what everybody else thinks?" she says. "Of course, I care about what other people think, but I'm just not that worried about how I come off to other people, and that's useful. I also don't take anything so seriously that I can't joke about it."

In 2022, Amy and her family relocated to Costa Rica, where she continues to research, report, host, and produce climate podcasts.

In one of the podcasts that Amy colaunched with climate essayist Mary Annaïse Heglar—called *Hot Take*—they're able to laugh at the absurdity in the climate movement sometimes.

Follow Amy Westervelt Online

Website: https://www.amywestervelt.com

Twitter: @amywestervelt

Instagram: @realamywestervelt

Critical Frequency: https://criticalfrequency.org/

Twitter: @CriticalFreqPod

Instagram: @criticalfrequency

Podcasts:

Host: @WeAreDrilled

Cohost: @realhottake

Wanjiku "Wawa" Gatheru: Black Girl Environmentalist

Wanjiku "Wawa" Gatheru is redefining the legacy of environmentalism.

In 2019 Wawa became the first Black person in history to receive the prestigious Rhodes, Truman, and Udall Scholarships.

"I've felt, as a Black girl, that being in the environmental space has often been traumatizing," Wawa says.

Before applying for the Rhodes Scholarship—the oldest graduate scholarship in the world—she dove into researching it first. "I began to understand that Cecil Rhodes was a racist, colonialist, and imperialist, and an awful man," she says about Rhodes, who was a rabid British supremacist, a wounding history that still plagues Black South Africans.

Wawa points out the paradox: Black and Brown people experience the most devastating and harmful effects from the climate crisis, but they're not the ones making the decisions to alleviate these issues. "I don't think you can be a leader without reckoning with the history of the very resources that you are choosing to tap into," Wawa says.

"I really struggled with this," she adds. "And I think I will continue to struggle with this. I don't believe that you can begin to even think of applying to something like the Rhodes Scholarship, without beginning to reckon with that legacy." Wawa is using her scholarships to pursue a graduate degree in nature, society, and environmental governance.

Wawa is the daughter of Kenyan immigrants who moved to the United States to make a better life for their children. She grew up in a rural, White town in Connecticut called Pomfret, which she says is "arguably one of the most beautiful places in the state of Connecticut and New England."

Her family—her parents, two sisters, and a brother—was the only Black family in her town. Her parents come from generations of farmers in Kenya. She has fond memories of her mom starting a huge garden on the plot of land next to their home, where they grew vegetables that went right into the amazing Kenyan meals she grew up on.

"My parents never talked about the climate crisis growing up," Wawa says. Nor did she see Black people represented in environmental spaces, like hiking, camping, or working in nature centers that she visited on school field trips.

"I personally never really saw myself as an environmentalist growing up," Wawa says. When she read or heard about the environment, it was usually centered around White people.

"I never saw myself represented," Wawa says, adding, "At this point, I had no conception of climate, it was all environmental or rather environmentalism."

She grew up surrounded by green space and the wilderness, but the environmental movement seemed like an ivory tower. It was such a space of privilege and power. "I never saw myself represented in the way environmentalism was presented to me, even though it literally surrounded me."

She envisioned herself becoming a doctor. "My parents are immigrants from Kenya, and I feel like a lot of African immigrant parents are like, 'Doctor, engineer, lawyer, choose!' I was like, 'Okay, I'll be a doctor.'"

She signed up to take chemistry but didn't like it. "I was literally the worst chemistry student you've ever met!" she jokes.

That's how, at age 15, Wawa ended up dropping chemistry to take the only other science class available: on environmental science. "I wasn't supposed to be in that class, but I fell in love with the course because my teacher actually added an environmental justice chapter."

One day in her high school environmental studies class changed Wawa's life. Her teacher cued up a TEDx talk by Peggy Shepard, a Black environmental justice organizer who'd been advocating for Black and Latinx communities in New York City for decades.

Wawa had never heard of her work. She listened intently as Peggy talked about how air pollution has had an impact on Black and Latinx youth, and how the asthma rates in these communities are so much higher compared to white communities.

Wawa says this was the moment she "connected the dots between race, class, gender, and our identities and how we experience the environment."

"I was like, 'Why is no one talking about this in my family? Why is it that environmentalism has always been presented to me as this very white issue that didn't involve me?' But now, I'm learning that it has everything to do with me and everything to do with my future."

In response to Plastic-Free July, a global movement that envisions a world free of plastic, Wawa wrote an essay for *Glamour* magazine called "Want to Be an Environmentalist? Start with Antiracism." "If communities of color are experiencing the worst of plastic pollution and the dynamics that make it possible, why aren't their stories centered in the conversations surrounding the problem?" Wawa asks.

In this essay, Wawa also quotes climate justice essayist Mary Annaïse Heglar, who she says is one of her inspirations. (Read more on Mary in chapter 2, about Amy Westervelt.) Mary describes existential exceptionalism, "which she explains as the tendency for the movement to see existential threats like climate change and racism as contending and unrelated.

BIPOC [Black, Indigenous, and people of color] may feel like environmentalism—as a concept—is unrelated to issues that pertain to our lives."

"As a Black environmentalist, I can confirm," Wawa writes. "While I grew up caring about the environment and issues like plastic pollution, I simply did not see myself as an 'environmentalist.' For the majority of my life, the term sat in an ivory tower of power, privilege, and whiteness and felt inaccessible and unrelated to my well-being. While I now know this to be untrue, the exclusivity of the community remains."

Wawa says that Mary writes about climate change in a way that makes her feel like her climate story was valid. "A lot of the frustration that I have from having to force my narrative into spaces isn't just out of anger; it's also out of love. And it's out of love for my family and friends who are Black and Brown."

Environmental justice is what inspired Wawa to focus on environmental studies when she went to the University of Connecticut. Still, during her four years in college, Wawa says that her professors rarely talked about environmental justice. She learned about the history of environmental movements to protect nature and wilderness in America, but her professors did *not* talk about the exclusion of poor people and people of color from these lands.

"It is no secret that the environmental movement's history is red with the blood of Indigenous genocide," Wawa wrote in another essay for *Vice* called "It's Time for Environmental Studies to Own Up to Erasing Black People."

Some of the people we think of as "the founding fathers" of the environmental movement were racist. "Many of the movement's founding fathers, such as Madison Grant, John Muir, and Aldo Leopold, were white supremacists that created the language of conservation to accommodate racialized conceptions of nature."

"If we're going to create equitable programs to try to ensure that all people have equal access to public land and green space, we need to be cognizant about the way that white supremacy serves as a deterrent, even if it's not as visible for people who don't experience colorism or colorist statements directed to them," Wawa says.

Wawa's *Vice* essay went viral. "So many women and girls and nonbinary girls reached out to me," she says. "They said to me, 'This is the first time I've seen myself as a Black environmentalist. This is the first time I've seen myself on paper. This is the first time I've seen myself in an article.'"

This is how she found herself in the public eye, agreeing to interviews, even if public speaking is something that terrifies Wawa. "I just mask it well. I used to cry before (or during) most public presentations before I turned 17. I am still working on speaking more confidently."

In 2020, after Wawa graduated from the University of Connecticut with a bachelor of arts in environmental studies and a minor in urban and community studies, she got the chance to interview her inspiration, Peggy Shepard!

Wawa told Peggy how much she has looked up to her. "Your work has really paved the way and has been a part of the blueprint of what the environmental justice movement is and what it will continue to blossom into."

Peggy pointed out that, unfortunately, there's still so much racism in our society. "What has changed is a little more consciousness about it, but it has not changed deeply yet."

Today, Wawa's mission is to change this. She's determined to bring Black climate activists to the front and center of conversations and decisions. Often, she is still the only Black person speaking on panels or at conferences.

"This is still something that I work through to this day," she says. "I find that if we're going to create equitable programs to try to ensure that all people have equal access to public land and green space, we need to be cognizant about the way that White supremacy serves as a deterrent. I do this work out of survival. I think so many Black girls do. It's necessary."

In 2021 Wawa founded Black Girl Environmentalist, an intergenerational community of Black girls, women, and nonbinary environmentalists. Her goal is to showcase the universality of Black girls, women, and nonbinary folk in the environmental space. "We are grounded by the values of environmental justice and understand that there is no such thing as a just climate future that doesn't center our unique lived experiences and knowledge systems."

During the pandemic 22-year-old Wawa launched the Reclaiming Our Time campaign to highlight Black climate activists at the forefront of addressing the climate crisis. "We are at the forefront right now of the climate crisis, yet our work is rarely centered or highlighted," Wawa says about the largest Black youth-led environmental initiatives seen in years.

"I don't think there's such a thing as an equitable climate future without centering on Black voices—not just the most vulnerable as a stagnant term, but the people who are experiencing climate change right now."

Where Are the Trees in Black Neighborhoods?

If you drive through any city in the United States—such as Oakland, Baltimore, Dallas, Denver, Miami, Portland, and New York—you'll notice the lack of trees in neighborhoods where families of color live.

These segregated neighborhoods have fewer trees, owing to racist governmental policies. Decades of racist policies in housing mean that during any heat wave, communities of color might be 5 to 20 degrees Fahrenheit hotter in the summer compared to the wealthier, Whiter neighborhoods in the same city. Black and Brown neighborhoods in the United States also experience much higher pollution than White communities.

Organizations like Groundwork USA are planting community gardens and urban farms in cities like Richmond in California, New Orleans, and Atlanta. They're also making greenways for walking and biking and restoring habitat and waterways.

In Chicago, Openlands is a nonprofit that's planting more trees in the most polluted neighborhoods on the South and West Sides. "To address the climate crisis, we not only need to cut emissions and transition our economy to clean energy, but we also must put carbon back in the ground," according to Openlands. "Forests, natural areas, parks, farmland, and open spaces all have the capacity to absorb large amounts of greenhouse gases from the atmosphere through plants and trees, returning carbon to the soil."

Unfortunately, many do not survive in these communities because of the abundance of pollutants in the air, according to Cheryl Johnson, executive director of People for Community Recovery, an environmental advocacy group based in Altgeld Gardens Homes on Chicago's far South Side.

This is why climate is so connected to justice and equity. In 2020 Openlands joined a lawsuit against the city of Joliet, Illinois. They've been fighting against the Illiana tollway, which wants to pave over thousands of acres of prime farmland and federally protected wildlife at Midewin National Tallgrass Prairie.

Wawa flew to England to begin her studies at Oxford in the fall of 2020, specifically to focus on making environmental education more accessible and relevant to people of color. "I will do a dissertation here, and I will be focusing on how colorism serves as a deterrent and a barrier for Black girls and women to want to partake in outdoor recreation and outdoor education and want to spend extended time outside."

The pandemic was spreading rapidly around Europe and the world, so Wawa had to stay isolated in her room at Oxford. During the rare moments she left her dorm, she noted that Oxford is "a very picturesque" town, but "there aren't many Black people. There aren't many Black Americans on top of that."

Wawa flew home to spend the holidays with her family in Connecticut. Because of COVID-19, she couldn't return to England, so she finished her grad classes online. That's when she found out that she'd been recognized as a Revolutionary Power fellow at the US Department of Energy, to add yet another feather to her cap of achievements.

"I decided to dedicate my life to environmental justice when I made the connection that while the climate crisis is the biggest threat to Black life, we are being sidelined in the very movement tasked with solving it," Wawa says. "It is precisely our proximity to climate injustice that makes us the most qualified to lead. We are already leading on solutions to survive.

"I have made the choice to do what I can in my lifetime to reframe and reimagine a legacy," Wawa adds.

Follow Wanjiku "Wawa" Gatheru Online

Website: https://www.wawagatheru.org/

Twitter: @wawagatheru

Instagram: @wawa_gatheru

Trimita Chakma:
Rising Up in the Global South

"Greta Thunberg's work is really important, but she's still representing the Global North," says Trimita Chakma, referring to the young Swedish climate activist who first caught the world's attention in 2018.

It's the people in the Global South who remain the most vulnerable to the devastating effects of the climate crisis. "This is where the climate change issues are at the forefront," Trimita observes. "This is where people are drowning."

The *Global South* refers to low-income countries in Latin America, Asia, Africa, and Oceania that are often socially or politically marginalized. The Global South is usually used as a metaphor to refer to low-income countries in relation to current global inequalities between countries, rather than geographical location, Trimita explains.

These are regions outside Europe and North America, and activists like Trimita point out that world leaders have historically dismissed the people in the Global South, who are the least responsible for global emissions.

Trimita describes herself as "a feminist activist and researcher." She was born and raised in Bangladesh, "but I'm not Bengali like most Bangladeshis," she says. "I belong to an ethnic minority in Bangladesh, and we're known as the Chakmas," explaining that she's a Chakma Indigenous woman from the Chittagong Hill Tracts (CHT).

CHT is located in southeastern Bangladesh, a very remote and hilly region that borders India and Myanmar. A total of 13 Indigenous groups live there, and each community has its own language, culture, traditions, and identity.

Some of the communities have no way to get to main roads or transportation. Most have no Internet connection. People here used to make their living by swidden or shifting cultivation, in which you clear land by slashing and burning vegetation.

"In the past, when Indigenous peoples had access to abundant land, they rotated the areas of cultivation each year," Trimita notes. "They mostly cultivated for their household consumption. They did not take more than what they needed to survive, which helped to maintain the ecosystem."

The nutrients in the land would return after a few years, but today Indigenous peoples have to survive with limited natural resources on such small areas of land, so it's very challenging to support their families. "Due to the increasing dispossession of land and resources caused by conflict, land grabbing, and climate change, their livelihoods have become highly vulnerable," Trimita says.

Furthermore, the Bangladesh government has settled hundreds of thousands of Bengali people in the CHT, and they now make up the majority of the population in the region. The military dictatorship in the late 1970s and 1980s forced Indigenous groups off their land against their will.

Growing up, Trimita's father traveled around the country for work, which meant that Trimita bounced around to different schools.

"I virtually ended up being the only Chakma kid in my class in every school I went to," she says. "It was easy to stereotype me due to my distinct appearance. Kids would often chant 'Chakma! Chakma!' if they saw me pass by. Sometimes I would be asked whether my people ate frogs and snakes, lived naked in the jungle, or spoke Chinese. These things upset me back then. It felt awful to be different, and I did not exactly embrace my Chakma identity with a sense of pride or happiness."

Trimita was about to start middle school when her parents said they wanted to send her and her sisters to an all-girls military school. She applied and got in. "It was a boarding school, very competitive, strict, and tough. It was run by the army and subsidized by the government, with a culture of punishment," she recalls. "I wouldn't send any kids I know there. But it made me very resilient to bullying. It didn't break me."

Trimita was 15 when her dad handed her an advertisement for a scholarship at United World Colleges (UWC), an international network of high schools that was founded in 1962 by the German educationalist Kurt Hahn, who envisioned engaging young people from all nations coming together to break down political, racial, and socioeconomic barriers and learn from one another.

She applied and earned a full scholarship. "I was one of the few students to be selected from a Bengali medium school to study at a UWC on scholarship."

This experience was unlike anything Trimita had ever gone through before. "It was the opposite of my military boarding school," she says. "We didn't have any uniforms, and we had a lot of personal freedom."

Trimita loved that you could dye your hair any color without fear of being punished. Students were not expected to conform to heternormative ideologies and were taught to value diversity and community service. "This was also my entry point to understanding justice and to see that the world is bigger than what I was experiencing in Bangladesh," she reflects.

"I was finally able to embrace my multiple identities—as a Chakma, as a woman, as a Bangladeshi, and as a global citizen," adding that she met students from 90 different countries! "My roommates were from England, Namibia, and Germany. I became best friends with a girl from Montenegro and had a crush on a boy from Lithuania, even though I had never heard of their countries before."

Trimita loved science and math, and she dreamed about becoming an astronaut: "In Germany, I studied electrical engineering and computer science. I was the only woman in my class who majored in computer science." Having *never* used a computer growing up, Trimita is clearly a fast learner! "No one that I knew in Bangladesh had computers back then."

After completing her undergraduate degree, Trimita went back to her hometown in the Chittagong Hill Tracts and worked for the United Nations, where she developed computer software. In her free time, she volunteered at Moanoghar, a local boarding school for disadvantaged Indigenous children, to provide computer training for their staff. Thanks to another scholarship from Australia, she landed at Carnegie Mellon University and earned a master's degree in information technology (IT) management. Upon her return to Bangladesh she worked as an IT manager, while in her free time she volunteered at a human rights organization for Indigenous peoples of Bangladesh called the Kapaeeng Foundation.

Through her volunteer work, she was determined to bring justice to the women and girls who'd been subjected to sexual violence in the Chittagong Hill Tracts for decades. "The young girls in my community were getting raped because of conflict over land, which is very common for Indigenous women everywhere," Trimita says.

Trimita also wanted women to heal. She wanted them to know that they're not alone. She also wanted the rest of the world to stand up and do something. That's why she, along with her friends, decided to bring *The Vagina Monologues* to Bangladesh. *The Vagina Monologues* is a play written by an activist named V (formerly Eve Ensler) that is based on dozens of interviews she had with women about their sexuality and their experiences with rape and abuse.

"When we started *The Vagina Monologues* it was already being performed in more than 140 countries," Trimita says. But this was something new for Bangladesh. The mission of *The Vagina Monologues*, part of the V-Day campaign, is to demand an end to violence against all women, girls, and the planet.

"The reaction was overwhelmingly positive," says Trimita. "Especially from older women who really appreciated the openness. The response from men was also very encouraging, and some of them have been our strong supporters."

Trimita decided she wanted to become a full-time feminist activist. So she left her IT job and accepted a lower-paying job at the Asia Pacific Forum on Women, Law and Development. Her first assignment was to organize grassroots activists from Asia to go to the COP20 in Lima, Peru. COP stands for Conference of the Parties, referring to the 197 nations that agreed to a new environmental pact, the United Nations Framework Convention on Climate Change, at a meeting in 1992.

"I realized that climate justice is a feminist issue," she says. "My entry point into climate was as a feminist activist."

Since her teenage years, Trimita has lived, studied, and traveled all around the world. Her mission is to help women rise up, especially in the Asia-Pacific, where women, in particular, suffer the effects of climate change.

So far, Trimita has worked with more than 85 grassroots communities across 22 countries! She was one of the main organizers of One Billion Rising when she lived in Bangladesh.

One Billion Rising

In 2022 One Billion Rising campaigned for the rise "for the bodies of all women, girls and the earth."

Their platform announces: "We are experiencing the devastating consequences of the ongoing vicious systems of patriarchy, imperialism, capitalism and racism on the world today. We see this destructive battle for power fought over women's bodies and the body of the earth. The devastation cannot be ignored."

Throughout the world, women are disproportionately affected by climate change. Extreme weather events such as droughts and floods have a greater impact on the most vulnerable—70 percent of the world's poor are women.

Women, especially, also have the knowledge and understanding of what is needed to adapt and change.

Today, Trimita is the foster mom of a boy named Parao Mro, who was born into a family from another hill tribe in her home region. His family was displaced from their traditional land. She explains that "it's very common especially with tobacco farms pushing tribes further into the jungle."

He'd been found at age six, wandering the hills alone. "His father died in a gunfight, and we never found his family again," she says. Trimita stepped in to make sure he had a home, and to pay for him to go to Moanoghar, the boarding school where she used to volunteer.

In Seoul, South Korea, Trimita is working and back in school. She works part-time at a global trade union federation that protects frontline workers and fights for a just transition to renewable energy. She is also engaged in facilitating feminist participatory action research projects for youth activism in Kiribati and Fiji.

She's also studying for a *second* master's degree in Asian women's studies. "I'd had it with information technology," she laughs. "I picked this program in Seoul because they were offering the Asian women's studies, not just 'women's studies.' I wasn't interested in the Western narrative on feminism because we already know that, right?"

Her two sisters—who live in Boston, Massachusetts, and Toronto, Canada, where they're both pursuing PhDs—describe Trimita as "committed, resistant, and persistent."

The description is spot-on.

Follow Trimita Chakma Online

Website: https://www.trimita.com

Twitter: @trimita

Trailblazer: Hunter Richards

Hunter Richards is a civil and environmental engineer in Boston, Massachusetts. She's also the first woman in her family to graduate from college.

Hunter grew up on a farm in rural Michigan. When she was in third grade, a young woman came into her class to help out, and Hunter connected with her. "She was with us throughout the year, and then she told us that she wouldn't be there anymore because was going to college," Hunter says.

"We were all kind of sad that we wouldn't see her anymore," Hunter remembers. "And then she explained what college was. I'd never really heard about college before then."

Around this time, Hunter watched the TV show *Gilmore Girls* with her mom, and she was fascinated about the main character Rory Gilmore's journey as she applied to college. "That's when I decided that I was going to go to Harvard one day," Hunter shares—the same school Rory always had her heart set on.

Then she learned how expensive college is. She knew that to have a shot, she'd need to study hard and get some significant financial support. Hunter's high school didn't offer AP Physics or AP Calculus, so she went to her physics and calculus teachers and asked to do independent study. She also got into a summer program at MIT.

In her senior year of high school, Hunter got into Harvard! In addition to studying, she held three jobs every semester: "I had to make money to pay my own bills and send money home to help out family."

She decided to major in engineering. "Growing up, I didn't know a single scientist or engineer," Hunter says. "I was so shocked to find out what an engineer was, and I couldn't believe that people would actually *pay* me to do math and science all day! As a woman in engineering, it's still pretty common to be the only woman in the room, but it's empowering to help make space for more women."

Hunter graduated from Harvard with a bachelor of science in engineering sciences, with a focus on environmental science and engineering. She likes to say, "Bob the Builder's got nothing on me!"

Environmental engineers protect people from adverse environmental effects, such as air pollution and contaminated water. They use engineering, soil science, biology, and chemistry to come up with solutions for environmental problems.

Today, Hunter is often the only woman on a job site. And the youngest. Moreover, she's five foot four and frequently surrounded by contractors who are six foot and taller. "It can be a big issue when you show up places and nobody takes you seriously as an engineer," she says.

Finding the right gear for the job is not always easy, either. Hunter has gone from store to store, for instance, searching for steel-toed boots in her size.

Hunter also speaks openly about being a queer engineer. "It turns out girls don't do engineering just to meet boys, after all," she jokes. "As a bisexual woman in STEM, I've struggled with how feminine I present and how people will perceive me. It's only now that my long-term partner is a man that I've realized how much I used to hide. . . . But the more we bravely open up, the more welcoming things become."

5

Tori Tsui:
Bad Activist

One morning, Tori Tsui's phone was blowing up with messages from friends, asking if they'd seen the news about "the Activist."

Tori followed the links to a series being promoted by CBS, in which activists would be pitted against each other in pursuit of funding for their causes. Celebrities like Usher were supposed to be the judges.

This has to be a joke. But the news confirmed otherwise.

"Companies like CBS and their shareholders think we are too incompetent to notice that they've run out of things to sell," Tori says. "So, now they're selling our pain back to us."

Tori points out that the entertainment industry targets youth who have limited resources, and they probably hadn't even asked any activists to weigh in on a show that would turn people's survival and trauma into entertainment.

"They offer us grant money, brand deals, exposure on prime time television," Tori says. "These are active efforts to make a mockery out of peoples' struggle. They think that if they put on *The Hunger Games*, we will calm down."

Most days begin early in Tori's apartment in Bristol, England, where they log online with a strong cup of coffee to prep for whatever the world might have in store.

"The busiest intersectional climate activist in the world." That's how the media has described Tori. It's true. Every day, Tori's phone buzzes with *so many* requests for interviews and speaking engagements that an agency now handles them. Tori is an incredible collaborator and coordinator.

Tori was born in New Zealand and raised in Hong Kong. Tori moved to England to get a degree in ecology and conservation. They know what it's like to be ignored for the color of their skin, or not represented in the mainstream, or even tokenized as "a Bond girl." They've spoken openly about navigating their Eurasian identity, and the racism they've faced much of their life.

Academia wasn't the right fit. So, Tori set their sights on making natural history documentaries.

"This is the home of the wildlife filmmaking industry and BBC. I moved to Bristol in hopes of becoming a wildlife filmmaker, and then I kind of went, *Oh, I'll be a climate activist instead.*" Tori laughs. "It's a beautiful, creative, and incredibly progressive city, as far as progressive cities go."

Around this time, on October 31, 2018, a group called Extinction Rebellion organized its first major protest on Parliament Square in London to announce a Declaration of Rebellion against the UK Government. British activists sat down in the road to block traffic at one of the city's most active intersections for more than two hours, to draw attention to the climate crisis.

The next few weeks were a whirlwind, according to Extinction Rebellion. "Six thousand rebels converged on London to peacefully block five major bridges across the Thames. Trees were planted in the middle of Parliament Square, and a hole was dug there to bury a coffin representing our future. Rebels super-glued themselves to the gates of Buckingham Palace as they read a letter to the queen. Extinction Rebellion was born.

In a letter published in the *Guardian* in 2018, a group of almost 100 scientists and academics declared their support for Extinction Rebellion, explaining, "If we continue on our current path, the future for our species is bleak."

Tori says that's when they made the decision to dedicate their life to activism instead of wildlife photography and videography.

They made a few short videos for Extinction Rebellion's social media channel on the impact of the climate crisis on certain species. Then Stella McCartney's creative director called Tori. Stella McCartney—an English fashion designer and daughter of singer-songwriter Sir Paul McCartney—had noticed Tori's work and wanted to make an offer.

Stella wanted Tori and some of the activists from Extinction Rebellion to model her winter line for a film that was written by author Jonathan Safran Foer and narrated by primatologist Jane Goodall.

In 2019 COP25 was supposed to take place in Santiago, Chile. Stella McCartney sponsored Tori's journey to sail for three months from Europe to the UN Climate Change Conference. The campaign was called Sail to the COP.

This group of youth activists was sailing instead of flying to make a statement about airplane emissions. But unfortunately, civil unrest in Chile that year forced COP25 to relocate to Spain—after the team had sailed halfway across the Atlantic.

They made the best of it and sailed to the Caribbean, where the team worked remotely to campaign for sustainability in the travel industry.

In 2020 the United Nations canceled the Climate Change Conference because of the COVID-19 pandemic, but the next year Unite for Climate Action was born.

In fall 2021 Tori organized a campaign to raise funds to get Latin American and Caribbean climate activists to COP26, the 26th annual climate change conference in Glasgow, Scotland. "I'm trying to get diverse voices represented," Tori says, explaining that the people most affected by climate change need to be at the center of climate policy.

The problem is, the leaders making critical decisions that shape our future (namely, White men) aren't listening, or responding to the climate emergencies all around us. "I was exhausted before COP26 even started. Burnt out from weeks of back-to-back actions and conferences, calls, jobs, and engagements," Tori says. "Why do we put so much emphasis on ourselves as sole individuals to do the work? It's not what I believe, it's not how change happens in the long run."

Tori describes the mood after they left COP26 as "bereft of joy and energy. . . . I feel robbed of energy and time and healing."

"I'm incredibly sensitive as a person, and I'm proud of this," Tori says. "I wouldn't be doing the line of work I'm doing if I wasn't sensitive. And I think it's what makes me happy, too, even if it's such a turbulent and stressful realm to work in."

Tori coproduces a podcast called *Bad Activist* (on Instagram @badactivistcollective). The podcast includes interviews with change-makers, artists, storytellers, and activists who are "trying to be a perfect activist in an utterly imperfect world."

"My humanity is rooted in a fundamental existence of knowing that I won't be perfect in a truly imperfect world," Tori says. "It is also inevitable that my ill mental health (often a symptom of the world we live in, my innate biology and traumas) and neurodivergence set me up to fail. I will never ever be anything that movements or people or strangers or society expect me to be."

Tori is also writing a book called *It's Not Just You* to unpack "how we speak about mental health and eco anxiety. Often the conversations are only focused on the individual, as opposed to the systems that we live in."

Tori speaks openly about living with borderline personality disorder, and about taking medication (sertraline, aka Zoloft) to take good care of themselves. "My head is such a noisy place," Tori says. "And I also find that my body's so sedentary sometimes, and I become so wrapped up in my thoughts. I'm somebody who, unfortunately, by virtue of the job that I'm doing at the moment, I spend a lot of time sitting at my desk."

That's why Tori makes sure to get out the door every day, to walk and move. They also love spending time with their partner, whom they describe as "somebody I met when I was at college," and is a constant loving support. "He was also studying conservation science. . . . He's somebody who has really allowed me to grow into my own. He's the kind of person that tries to understand me without trying to impose his own views on things like, who I am or who I should be. And it's really healing to be with somebody like that."

Tori also opens up about what anxiety means to them. "Far too often, when I see articles about eco anxiety, they give these tips to deal with eco anxiety, like do yoga and meditate. That's great. But are those just temporary solutions? Are we just slapping a Band-Aid on the problem?"

We all need to remember to take care of ourselves, Tori says. "I think it's so important to remember that activists aren't just activists, and they like to spend time being human in some way. So yeah, it's just a gentle reminder to find joy as well."

Tori loves the Netflix show *Shadow and Bone*, especially when they're snuggled up with their partner. "The protagonist is a Bristol-based actress named Jessie Mei Li, and she's half-Chinese and half-English, like me! Much like myself. Her dad is from Hong Kong, and I'm like, *Who is this person?* We never see people like me on screen. I'm like already a huge fan of hers, and she lives here. I want to be her friend."

Tori also loves to read, paint, and craft. They make bright, beautiful earrings for sale on Etsy @ByToriTsuiunder with the tagline "Earrings for social and climate justice cause."

In 2021 all the proceeds that Tori earned went straight to supporting Unite for Climate Action to get Latin American and Caribbean youth to the UN Climate Conference COP26.

In the meantime, on account of the pandemic, Tori has not been able to visit their family at home in Hong Kong for three years.

From their home in England, Tori continues to rise up every week to work. "It's understandable that many people don't know what to do or don't know where to start when it comes to facing the climate crisis. It can be so overwhelming, but I just keep saying, 'Lean into it and you will find your flow. You will find a way. We can work together on this.'"

Trailblazer: Mitzi Jonelle Tan

A climate justice activist in Metro Manila, Philippines, Mitzi Jonelle Tan has a stark message for "the world leaders, fossil fuel companies, multinational companies and richest, especially of the Global North": "You have caused this climate crisis. Your greed for profit has caused the death of people in my community and millions across the globe already, and it will continue to get worse and impact your communities, too, if you do not start treating this crisis like a crisis. We need drastic emission cuts and reparations for adaptation and loss and damages now."

Mitzi started striking for the climate because the Philippines is the second-most vulnerable country to the climate crisis, she says. "Yet our contribution to the global greenhouse gas emissions is so minimal."

Mitzi was a 20-year-old college student when she got the opportunity to talk to a Lumad Indigenous leader in the Philippines. "That's when I truly understood the need for collective action in whatever means necessary to address the systemic nature of the climate crisis," she says. "He was telling us about how they were being displaced, harassed, militarized, and killed."

That was the moment that Mitzi decided to organize her friends to form the Youth Advocates for Climate Action Philippines (YACAP). "We realized that there was a need for a youth climate movement in the Philippines, and so we started YACAP."

Mitzi's mission is to make sure that voices from the Global South are heard, amplified, and given space. "I am an activist because I don't want to be afraid anymore. I don't want to ever again be afraid of drowning in my own bedroom because of the floods," she says. "I am an activist because of my deep love for the people and the environment, a love that binds me to the movement calling for climate and social justice."

Since 2019 Mitzi has been raising awareness, talking to policymakers, and organizing strikes. Mitzi is also active with Fridays for Future, the group started by Greta Thunberg. She has spent days and weeks meeting with Indigenous people, farmers, and other stakeholders in the Philippines to learn about their experiences and amplify their campaigns for justice.

In 2021 Mitzi traveled to Glasgow, Scotland, to attend COP26 when more than 20,000 heads of state, diplomats, and activists joined together for the most critical climate talks of our lifetimes.

It was a critical opportunity for leaders around the globe to make drastic actions to slow down catastrophic environmental collapse. Mitzi was disappointed and exhausted. "So far, this #COP26 is just like all the ones in the past: exclusive and ignoring the voices of the most marginalized," she says, explaining that these leaders have made promises for years but have not followed through with real action.

She said that Global North countries "continue to ignore their historical responsibility both for the climate crisis and their exploitation of our lands as they erase any forms of accountability and blame those they exploit for 'not doing enough.'" Mitzi says that people who rise up for change keep her going. "The activists who I've known online for so long and the love I have in my heart for them, that's where my hope is."

Trailblazer: Aryana Henthorne

"Aren't we the stewards who've kept the system going until now?" asks Aryana Henthorne, a member of the Sherwood Valley Band of Pomo Indians in Mendocino, California.

Aryana is referring to the generations of Indigenous people, like her family, who took care of the land for thousands of years until White colonists displaced and expelled them.

"We can't just be silenced anymore," says Aryana, who's currently getting her PhD in cell and molecular biology at the University of Hawai'i. "Climate change won't let us be silent."

One of Aryana's goals is food sovereignty, which means reclaiming the power of food. Access to food is a basic human right. Food sovereignty puts the "needs of those who produce, distribute and consume food at the heart of food systems and policies rather than the demands of markets and corporations."

Aryana and her community have been trying for years to regain access to their homeland on the coast of California, where salmon and red abalone used to be abundant. Thanks to coastal development, including roads and dams, wildlife has declined as they've lost their habitat.

Aryana says it's time for leaders at every level—global, federal, state, and local—to give Native people space to share aboriginal land management strategies and participate in the decision-making process. "Everyone, including Native people, should be in the room where decisions happen," she says.

Indigenous Peoples have spent many decades identifying the effects of the climate crisis related to food, such as environmental contamination and the loss of traditional knowledge as well as their traditional lands and resources. Yet many Indigenous people in the United States live in food apartheid.

"As an attorney who has practiced in Indian Country for most of my adult life, and as a Tribal citizen, I have seen the disproportionate difficulties Natives and Tribes have faced in agriculture," says Heather Dawn Thompson, director of USDA Office of Tribal Relations.

For decades, Heather, who lives in South Dakota, has seen the systemic barriers faced by Native American farmers and Tribal nations, including her own family, who's part of the Cheyenne River Sioux tribe.

This is why Indigenous people throughout the world are claiming their rights to control, protect, and restore their traditional food systems and sources.

Part II
Hold Fast to Science

6

Katharine Hayhoe:
The Science Mom Who's Saving Us

People have called Katharine Hayhoe a loony, a fraud, a clown.

Why? Because she's talking about climate change. "I'm attacked by trolls every single day," says Katharine, a climate scientist who's from Canada and now lives in West Texas where she's a professor in the Department of Political Science at Texas Tech University. She's also the chief scientist at The Nature Conservancy, a global organization that works in more than 70 countries and territories and all 50 states, where Katharine runs the science program.

"I know this is a total cliché, but whatever doesn't kill me makes me stronger. I sort of take it almost like a reverse compliment," she says. "If they took time out of their day to send me—somebody they don't even know—a really nasty email or social media message, I have to assume that they view me as a threat. And that means that I'm doing something right."

Katharine is an atmospheric scientist, meaning that she has spent much of her life studying the air around Earth.

"The bottom line is this: scientists have known since the 1850s that carbon dioxide traps heat," Katharine says. "It's been building up in the atmosphere from all the coal, oil, and gas we've burned since the start of the Industrial Revolution to generate electricity, heat our homes, power our factories, and, eventually, run our cars, ships, and planes."

It's undeniable that we, as humans, are responsible for global warming. "According to natural factors, the planet should be cooling, not warming," Katharine says. "We are the cause of all of the observed warming—and then some."

Katharine was born and raised in Ontario, Canada. She was studying physics and astronomy at the University of Toronto in Canada when she decided to take a class in climate science. "That class completely shocked me and ended up changing my life," she says. "I didn't realize climate science was based on the exact same basic physics—thermodynamics, nonlinear fluid dynamics, and radiative transfer—I'd been learning in astrophysics. And I definitely didn't realize that climate change wasn't just an environmental issue; it's a threat multiplier."

This means that climate change takes the "most serious humanitarian issues confronting climate change today—hunger, poverty, lack of clean water, injustice, refugee crises, and more—and it makes them worse. How could I not do everything I could to help fix this huge global challenge?"

After earning a bachelor of science in physics and astronomy from the University of Toronto, Katharine switched gears and headed to the University of Illinois at Urbana–Champaign to get her master's degree and later a PhD in atmospheric science. This is what led her to research how climate change was altering ecosystems in the Great Lakes and the water supply in California.

"People always talk about saving the planet," she says. "But the planet will be orbiting the sun long after we're gone."

The urgency, for her, was that human beings were in danger. And we are responsible for this.

"The impacts are serious, and the time to act is now," Katharine says. "Climate change is a human issue because it affects every single one of us; and every single one of us has a really important part to play in helping to fix it." This set Katharine on her life mission "to do everything I can to help fix it. I'm absolutely determined about that."

When Katharine's husband was offered a position as a linguistics professor at Texas Tech University, Katharine came along. "I ended up in Texas serendipitously because the university was recruiting my husband, and I was the 'plus one.' There are no other climate scientists for 200 miles!" she laughs. "And once I arrived, that's why I started to get invites to talk to people."

Katharine started teaching as a research professor in the geosciences department at Texas Tech University. She recalls her first class: "We had just moved to Lubbock, Texas, which had recently been named the second-most conservative city in the entire United States. A colleague asked me to guest teach his undergraduate geology class."

She showed up to the lecture hall, which she describes as "cavernous and dark" and tracked the history of the carbon cycle through geologic time to the present day. Students slumped over, dozing, or looked at their phones. "I ended my talk with a hopeful request for any questions. And one hand shot up right away. I looked encouraging, he stood up, and in a loud voice, he said, 'You're a Democrat, aren't you?'"

"No," she replied at once, "I'm Canadian."

Today, Katharine continues to work with cities, states, federal agencies, and businesses, helping them prepare for the impacts of a changing climate. She says that her research is like being the pilot for a big ship that's trying to get through a narrow passage. "Let's say that we're all on this large ship, and it's going through this strait with lots of rocks, which are like the climate risks. I have a specialized knowledge of these risks to help get the ship through. Because if we don't fix climate change, we're not going to be able to fix anything else."

Oh, and when Katharine isn't steering that ship, she's wearing a range of different hats:

- Teaching and working at Texas Tech University as the political science endowed professor in public policy and public law and a Horn distinguished professor
- Writing a ton! In addition to her book *Saving Us: A Climate Scientist's Case for Hope and Healing in a Divided World,* and another book on high-resolution climate projections she also wrote in 2021, Katharine was a lead author on four National Climate Assessments for the United States and has contributed chapters to books on topics ranging from environmental theology to climate solutions.
- Hosting the PBS digital series *Global Weirding*
- Speaking to audiences big and small about why climate change matters to them and what we can all do about it

"For the past 20 years, I've been working with cities, states, and federal agencies to figure out how to prepare for the impacts of a changing climate," she says. "And I don't just study climate change—I also talk about it."

You can find Katharine posting almost every day on Twitter, Instagram, and even TikTok. Local and national news often reach out to her for interviews. "I'll talk anywhere and to anyone."

During climate week, Jimmy Kimmel—the American late-night television host, comedian, writer, and producer—invited Katharine to talk about climate change on his show. He asked her what it's like to be a climate expert in the middle of the conservative big oil country, and how her evangelical beliefs intersect with climate science. The same week, she was mentioned by Seth Meyers on his late-night show and featured in a *New Yorker* profile.

"Because I try to fit in as much as possible, my days are super scheduled," Katharine says. "I have a Google Calendar that I live by that often fills up months in advance. And I make sure that my calendar has time for all my priorities, not just the urgent ones. This means that I schedule time to spend with the family, too."

Dinner together as a family is very important to Katharine. Her husband, Andrew Farley, is now an evangelical pastor and radio host. When he gets home from his call-in radio show—*The Grace Message*, which is live on Sirius XM every evening at 7 PM, central time—they have dinner with their teenage son.

"I try not to give an evening talk more than once a week because family time is in the evening," she says. "We eat together at the table, play games, and maybe watch something together."

"In my career, I think I'm proudest of how I've been able to communicate information that people can use in real life," Katharine says.

In addition to being a prominent climate scientist, Katharine is an incredibly engaging science communicator who "can convert nonbelievers—or, to put it in her terms, make people realize that they've believed in the importance of this issue all along." Writing for the *Washington Post*, Dan Zak observes, "She knows how to speak to oilmen, to Christians, to farmers and ranchers. She is a scientist who thinks that we've talked enough about science, that we need to talk more about matters of the heart."

Her TED talk on "The Most Important Thing You Can Do to Fight Climate Change" has been viewed over 5 million times. "So often, science is so abstract," Katharine explains. "But ever since I did my PhD, my research has focused on developing information that people can use to make real-life decisions, whether they are a water district planning for water demand and supply, or a power company trying to make sure that they can still supply electricity during heat waves. I just feel very fortunate, and very proud of the fact that I've been able to actively contribute to improving the quality of people's lives and helping real people."

Anthony Leiserowitz, director of the Yale Program on Climate Change Communication, says, "Katharine Hayhoe is a national treasure."

Thanks to her work and research on the human impacts to the climate, she's been recognized as one of the UN Champions of the Earth. *Time* magazine named her one of the 100 Most Influential People. *Fortune* magazine listed her as one of the World's 50 Greatest Leaders. *Working Mother* called her one of the 50 Most Influential Moms (an honor that she loves).

The list goes on and on. "These are all tremendous honors, for which I'm enormously grateful (and constantly surprised)," Katharine says. "What means the most to me personally, though, is when just one person tells me sincerely that they had never cared about climate change before, or even thought it was real; but now, because of something they heard me say, they've changed their mind. That's what makes it all worthwhile."

Global Weirding

Katharine writes and produces a PBS series called *Global Weirding* that you can also watch on YouTube.

"Global warming—an increase in the average temperature of the planet—isn't something we notice directly in our daily lives," Katharine says. "What we do notice, though, is *global weirding*."

"Climate change is the reason why unprecedented heat waves are baking the Pacific Northwest and thawing permafrost in the Arctic and Siberia. It's also why heavy precipitation events are increasing in frequency and severity, dumping record-setting levels of rainfall from Texas to Germany. As the oceans warm, tropical storms like hurricanes, cyclones, and typhoons are becoming stronger and intensifying faster, wreaking greater havoc around the world. Rising sea levels are inundating low-lying coastal areas from Bangladesh to the South Pacific to Miami. Longer, stronger droughts are ravaging East Africa and much of the western United States, and more intense wildfires are burning greater areas in places like Australia, British Columbia, and California."

Katharine addresses these issues on her show, and she answers lots of questions: How long do we have to save the Earth? Do plastics affect climate change?

For example, in her episode about "The Pandemic's Effects on Climate Change," Katharine explains: "This pandemic is responsible for untold suffering around the world. If anything, it's simply reminding us how interconnected we all are, and how we can ignore a crisis until it's brought to our attention. Let's take a step back and say, 'What is going on?'"

As an evangelical Christian, Katharine often speaks to religious communities. (The World Evangelical Alliance named her their climate ambassador!)

"What really changed my life, and my perspective, was when I realized that climate change is profoundly unfair," Katharine says. "It disproportionately affects the poorest and most marginalized people—the very people who've done the least to contribute to the problem. The statistics from Oxfam today are that the [3.1 billion] poorest people produce 7 percent of emissions, yet they are bearing the brunt of the impact. And that is absolutely not fair."

In her book *Saving Us: A Climate Scientist's Case for Hope and Healing in a Divided World,* Katharine describes how, when she was nine years old, her family moved from Canada to Colombia, where "my parents spent several years working at a bilingual school and helping out with a local church."

Her parents were missionaries and educators who'd travel on dirt roads to remote villages, where Katharine visited homes without running water or electricity. "In Colombia in the 1980s, life was challenging at the best of times: poverty, inequality, lack of clean water and health care; corruption and danger from the mafia, the guerrillas, the paramilitaries. . . . When disaster struck, it could be devastating. When rains came, entire neighborhoods were swept away. When drought hit, people starved."

She defines an evangelical as "someone who takes the Bible seriously," explaining that the more that she learns about science, the more her awe and faith in God increases. "I care about climate change because I'm a Christian," she says. "I believe that we have a responsibility to care for every living thing on the planet, and that we are to care about the least of these."

For an in-depth, personal profile the *New Yorker* ran about Katharine called "How to Talk About Climate Change Across the Political Divide," the journalist brought along her eight-year-old son for their interview after Katharine encouraged her to do so, explaining that her own son has joined her work trips since he was a baby. "Over the last decade there has been a huge revolution in terms of the level of childcare provided at scientific meetings, and in terms of people's attitudes about bringing your children along," Katharine says. "More often than not, other colleagues' response has been,

'Wow, you can do that?' And I feel like it's empowered them to be able to do it themselves."

Katharine loves witnessing how environmental action trickles down to younger generations. For example, her son Gavin now eats Beyond Meat, the plant-based meat, because he prefers it to beef for both the flavor and the environment.

Katharine spends a lot of time connecting to other parents. Especially mothers.

"Being a parent is pretty close to the middle of your heart," she says. "So, often, a lot of my conversations that I have with people are focused on being a parent, on the fact that we would do anything for our kids, and we want the best possible life for them. And we are worried about them. And that's why we care about climate change."

Here's why Katharine says she wrote *Saving Us:* "I'm fighting for climate action because of who and what I love, and I believe everyone else would, too, if they knew what was at stake. So that's why I wrote my book."

Writing this book "had been on my heart for years. It began more than a decade ago, when I started to be attacked by people who didn't like what I was saying," she says. "People I didn't know, who'd never met me, yet who thought that if they called me names and threatened me, they could silence me and shut me up."

"I love my son and all my nieces and nephews, I love my family, I love the place where I grew up and the place I live now. I love water and snow; I love people and science; I love God, and I love this amazing world we all share. Whoever you are, I know you have people and places you love, too. That's why, to care about climate change, we only have to be one thing, a human."

At the end of every day, Katharine and her family clean up after dinner, load the dishwasher, and head to bed. "Hope is what keeps me going," she says. "But hope isn't something that just sort of arrives. I've learned that hope is something you have to search for actively."

When Katharine sees real changes already happening, this also gives her hope. Especially when big companies like Apple or Walmart are transitioning to clean energy. Or when countries are making national changes to get power from solar and wind.

"Many universities and seminaries and large organizations are divesting," she says. "BlackRock, which is a huge investment firm that controls over seven trillion dollars, just announced they're divesting from coal, and it sent enormous tidal waves, not just ripples but tsunamis, throughout the financial world when they said that. So there really is action happening."

"I actually make a practice of hope," Katharine adds. "I go and I look for information that is helpful. And I share that information with people because other people need that too."

Follow Katharine Hayhoe Online

Website: https://www.katharinehayhoe.com

Twitter: @KHayhoe

Instagram: @katharinehayhoe

Jacquelyn Gill:
Lost in the Ice Age

It was the dream of a lifetime for Jacquelyn Gill to fly from the United States to the vast Arctic in northeastern Siberia with three other scientists and film the documentary *Lost Beasts of the Ice Age*.

That is, until Jacquelyn came close to losing her life.

The adventure started when Jacquelyn, a University of Maine professor of climate science and ecology, got an invitation to do fieldwork in the extreme north of Russia. She'd spent so many years studying it in books and journals, but she'd never actually visited in real life.

Jacquelyn spent months preparing for the trip to Russia's Republic of Sakha to study Ice Age fossils in the Siberian permafrost. She knew it would be physically demanding, so she trained every day by hiking with her dog and working out at the gym. She prepped her gear, critically including a bug net!

"I feel like I'm about to jump into a time machine!" Jacquelyn says. She could already picture tens of thousands of animals that had wandered here at one time and died.

From the get-go, the trip was tough. Every morning began with a daily four-hour boat ride with her colleagues, followed by another shorter boat ride, and then a hike up the river. After hours of sitting and then miles of walking, Jacquelyn made it to the site where woolly mammoths, woolly rhinos, wolves, and cave lions once roamed 30,000 years ago.

Because of global warming and the effects of more greenhouse gases in the atmosphere, the permafrost here is melting and exposing the frozen carcasses of the mammals that thrived here in the cold.

Locals drilled cave-like holes in the permafrost so Jacquelyn and the other scientists could explore and study the species underground. Jacquelyn had so many questions. Topping the list: How could so many animals survive in such a cold place?

Due to the frozen soil that is melting, she could see and examine these huge animals, which allowed her and other scientists to study their DNA from their mummified remains for the first time in history. They even discovered a cave lion cub that was still intact. "We actually call them mummies, not even fossils," Jacquelyn says, explaining that scientists like herself use the term *mummification* to refer to desiccated (dried-out) bodies that are unusually well preserved—they don't have to be from ancient Egypt! "They have skin, tissues, and even blood! They look like they could've died yesterday."

At one point in the film, Jacquelyn exclaims: "Oh my God!"

She describes these frozen caves as windows into an ecosystem from the past. "This is how we get to tell the story of climate change and changing ecosystems," she says. "I like to think about it in terms of forensics. If you're familiar with shows like *Bones* or *CSI*, we use a lot of the same exact tools. . . . Except instead of reconstructing a crime scene, we are reconstructing past environments through time."

The days were long and grueling. For ten days in a row, Jacquelyn got up at 6 AM and traveled hours to work the entire day without breaks. The long hours started to take their toll.

"We were finishing up in the field one day, and I was getting winded, which was strange, because I'd been training all summer." Even just walking to the bathroom would make her short of breath.

She thought that she was just exhausted. But on her way to catch her flight home, she struggled to breathe. She almost passed out on the runway.

"I had this thought, *I am not going to die here*," Jacquelyn recalls.

Blood tests confirmed that she had deep-vein thrombosis (a painful condition caused by a blood clot growing in a vein) in both legs, and large pulmonary embolisms (a potentially life-threatening condition that can occur when a blood clot breaks free and travels to the lungs, blocking blood flow) in both lungs. She felt grateful to the doctors, nurses, and her film producer for rallying around to support her. Oh, and also for health insurance.

Even so, upon returning to Maine six weeks later, Jacquelyn would say, "It was, hands down, one of the most incredible experiences of my life, and I can't wait to tell you all about it when the show airs."

Today, Jacquelyn is an associate professor of paleoecology and plant ecology at the School of Biology and Ecology and Climate Change Institute in Bangor, Maine. She's highly respected as a paleoecologist, starting with the paper she wrote as a young graduate student for *Science* about why mammoths in North America might have died when the last ice age ended.

Jacquelyn loves the challenge of summarizing her work in plain, straightforward language. Here's how she describes *exactly* what she does: "I study how trees and other living things responded during the many changes that took place as the world came out of the last ice age. Many large animals died out, the world became warmer, humans moved to new parts of the world for the first time, and living things began growing in places that had been under a thick layer of ice for a very long time. . . . By learning about how the world has responded to the changes of the past, we can better understand how living things may act as they face human-caused changes in the years to come."

Meteorologist Eric Holthaus, Jacquelyn's cohost on climate science podcast *Warm Regards*, says, "She's arguably just as talented at communicating science and its significance in clear and compelling ways."

Jacquelyn grew up in what she describes as rural, working-class towns. Her dad worked in steel, coal, and oil, and her mom was a nurse. "I'm the only academic in the family," Jacquelyn says, although she later learned that one of her uncles—who died before she was born—was a permafrost researcher. "I think my family is proud of me, although they don't necessarily understand what it's like being in academia."

Her father and stepfather both served in the US Navy. "It turns out, bouncing from place to place as a kid is a great way to instill an early fascination with our planet—everywhere we moved, I encountered new landscapes, new cultures, new climates, and new plants and animals."

One of her best childhood memories was visiting Acadia National Park in Maine, where she had an epiphany while standing knee-deep in a bog of mud: "I didn't just love science, I wanted to *do* science."

She went to College of the Atlantic in Bar Harbor, Maine, where Acadia National Park was practically in her backyard.

"I'm a scientist. But I wasn't born one," Jacquelyn said at the Rally to Stand Up for Science to a crowd of several thousand scientists in Copley Square in Boston.

Thanks to funding ($800,000!) from a National Science Foundation CAREER award, Jacquelyn is currently researching environmental change and extinction on the mammoth steppe, a cold and dry region—and also the most extensive biome on earth—that spans from Spain eastward across Eurasia to Canada and from the Arctic islands to China. Bison, horses, and woolly mammoths once roamed across the land and thrived.

"Herbivores remain some of the most threatened animals today, so understanding the 'Serengeti of the ice age' can help in the management of Earth's largest animals today and may provide insights into the role native grazers play in a warming Arctic," Jacquelyn writes.

Melting Arctic in Siberia Distresses Scientists

Permafrost is a permanently frozen layer below Earth's surface. It consists of soil, gravel, and sand, usually bound together by ice.

As the ground temperature warms, it weakens the frozen "cap" and fractures the tundra's fragile topsoil, which supports the mosses and shrubs that Arctic herbivores like reindeer graze on. Journalists on assignment in the Artic today have been reporting about craters ripping open in what used to the one of the coldest places on earth.

Scientists say the ongoing climate crisis will not spare Siberia. As permafrost thaws, it releases even more greenhouse gases responsible for global warming.

Jacquelyn says that if she were an animal, she'd be a climate musk ox. What's a musk ox? "Musk oxen are tough, resilient, ice age survivors," she says. "Musk oxen are matriarchal. They tough out the worst of the Arctic winter through sheer will. When one of their herds is vulnerable, the strong circle up and protect the weak, facing outwards like a circular phalanx of badassery."

Jacquelyn also describes herself as someone who "always had big feelings for people, the planet, and animals." She cares deeply about living beings, which means that she's often rolling up her sleeves to jump in and help out. "When it comes to the climate crisis, I'm *not* giving up. We need everyone to pitch in."

Follow Jacquelyn Gill Online

Website: https://contemplativemammoth.com

Twitter: @JacquelynGill

Instagram: @glacialdrift

Trailblazer: Beth Shapiro

Beth Shapiro is an incredible evolutionary biologist in Santa Cruz, CA.

Some people also call Beth a *paleobiologist*—someone who studies the biology of fossil animals and plants. In other words, she spends a lot of time analyzing ancient DNA.

"There's nothing that doesn't already have our fingerprint on it," says Beth, referring to the ways that humans have been manipulating nature for the past 50,000 years.

All our meddling has created turmoil on Earth. But now, thanks to biotechnology, we have the tools to start repairing. It's our responsibility to take care of our planet. It's time.

For example, now that we can engineer genomes of certain species, we can "help them adapt to drier soils, more acidic oceans, and more polluted streams," Beth says.

In her book *Life as We Made It: How 50,000 Years of Human Innovation Refined—and Redefined—Nature*, Beth writes about using "gene drives." This is a method that scientists use to accelerate the spread of favorable genetic traits in populations. Since the dawn of humanity, we have been crudely altering the genetics of our environment. Now, we have the knowledge and tools to shape our environment in more careful, thoughtful, and repairing ways.

"We have to become better gardeners of what's here," Beth says, explaining that we have the technologies to help species adapt, especially those nearing extinction.

But we need to be conscientious about the ways that we "meddle." In Beth's words,

> When I talk about meddling better, what I'm really thinking about is that the pace of habitat change and climate change in the world is faster now than evolution can keep up. Yet we have new technologies that we might be able to use to help species to adapt at a pace that keeps up with the changes to their habitat. We can use these technologies in agriculture, for example, to create foods that can grow in poor soils or challenging climates, that can grow faster, or that produce more edible stuff. And we can also use these technologies to help species that are threatened with becoming extinct.

Beth is a professor of ecology and evolutionary biology at University of California, Santa Cruz, and also a Howard Hughes Medical Institute investigator. (Her Twitter bio reads, "I still don't have a mammoth, but I do have a new book!")

She's very excited about the ways that gene-editing technologies can help us survive, whether we're helping corals thrive in warmer water or transferring genetic immunity to species that are nearing extinction, like black-footed ferrets.

When Beth isn't teaching or researching, she's running. Sometimes that means jogging around her neighborhood. Other times, it means chasing after her two young children. "I like to be outside," she says. "This place where we live is pretty spectacular."

Brigitte Baptiste: Queering Ecology

Brigitte Baptiste wakes up at 3 AM, tiptoes into her kitchen in Bogotá, Colombia, and makes herself an espresso. "I like strong coffee!" she laughs.

Her wife, Adriana, and their two daughters, Candelaria and Juana Pasión, are still asleep. So this is the only time of the day that Brigitte—an ecologist and renowned global expert on biodiversity—can steal a moment to read, research, and prepare for the day. Today happens to be a very big day: it's her two-year anniversary as rector of Universidad Ean, one of the most prestigious institutions of higher education in the country.

Brigitte is also the first-ever Colombian trans woman to be appointed as director of a university in Colombia. "I have 10 meetings a day, sometimes two or three meetings at the same time! From 3 to 6 AM is the only time I can write and plan," she says. "It's crazy. I need to lighten my agenda." By the time the sun rises, her phone is ringing, and her family is up, including her hungry cats. "But it's not boring at all. It's all amazing."

Brigitte confesses that she often falls asleep on the way home from her work office. "Don't worry, I'm not driving my electric car. Someone drives me home, and I sleep before having dinner with my family or visiting my mother and father."

Brigitte is an incredible multitasker. Her day might include writing a climate report for a global panel on biodiversity, presenting a new plan to the university to build an arts center, drafting a lecture that week on, say, "Queering Ecology," or writing her next column for *La República*, Colombia's economics newspaper.

Brigitte's love of ecology comes from traveling with her family when she was little. "My parents loved to drive around the country and camp outdoors. I had the opportunity to learn so much about the diversity of nature. I loved everything from watching ants climb to walking in the sand on the beach."

National Geographic once said that "if Earth's biodiversity were a country, it could be called Colombia." This country has the most diversity of bird and orchid species in the world, with plants, butterflies, freshwater fish, and amphibians coming in second in the world. There are more than 300 types of ecosystems in Colombia!

In the center of the country, you see the volcanoes and mountains of the Andes. Tropical beaches line the north and west. There are also deserts and vast grasslands, called Los Llanos. The southern part of the country has the dense forests of the Amazon basin, and the northwest has warm jungles called the Chocó, which reach across the Panama border. The jungle is home to an astonishing array of wildlife, from jaguars to poison dart frogs.

A Colombian tradition for families who can afford it is to send their kids to Disney World in Florida when they graduate from high school. This is when Brigitte went to the United States for her first time. She loved people watching as she walked around the amusement park.

Back home, Brigitte went to college and earned a biology degree. Then she was awarded a Fulbright, one of the most prestigious scholarships in the world, which allowed her to get her master's degree in Latin American Studies at the University of Florida in Gainesville. In college, she also founded an environmental nonprofit.

Back in Colombia, she traveled to the high Andes—the longest continental mountain range in the world—to work with local communities in forest management. Before her master's research, she had completed a biology thesis on the ecology of fisheries in the Amazon, after spending a year fishing with Indigenous tribes. She often reminds people that you learn about ecology by living it, not in textbooks.

After 15 years of teaching and researching at the Pontificia Universidad Javeriana in Bogotá—with a short break for a couple of years, studying in Barcelona—Brigitte became the director of the Alexander von Humboldt Biological Resources Research Institute, linked to the Ministry of the Environment, with the goal of protecting Colombian biodiversity.

Brigitte was 35 years old when she began transitioning. At this point, she was already highly respected for her work and accomplishments in academia. "When I was finally able to be myself, to become Brigitte, my career was already launched, and my CV spoke for me," she says.

She was considered to be one of the greatest experts on both environmental and biodiversity issues in Colombia when she came out as Brigitte. "When I give lectures around the world, sometimes two hundred people are waiting for me after class," she says.

"Mostly, they do not want to talk about plants in the jungle. Some want to know if I had a complete sex-change surgery. Others are searching for answers on questions of life. When you are a trans woman with my looks, you have no choice but to be open and honest about yourself. Colombia is a conservative country, where religion is dominant. The idea that you are free to choose who you want to be is appealing to many people."

Over the years, Brigitte has sustained attacks on social media, yet she has risen above the confrontation as a renowned climate leader in the world. (In 2016 Colombia became the fourth country in South America, a heavily Catholic region—after

Argentina, Uruguay, and Brazil—to legalize same-sex marriage. Ecuador and Costa Rica approved same-sex marriages in 2019 and 2020.)

The magazine *BELatina* profiled Brigitte as one of "Three Extraordinary Transgender Latinas You Should Know": "Her legacy has impacted biodiversity conservation, LGBTQ rights, and the way we think about business."

For Brigitte, trans identity is part and parcel of biodiversity. "The two are ultimately completely linked," she says. "I don't like labels, even less identity, we live in an ambiguous world and that seems great to me, because ambiguity calls for genius and creativity."

Brigitte has refused to let others bring her down. "Most of my life, I dressed in gray or brown colors, probably because that's how people dress in the mountains. It's cool here or rainy often. But when I became Brigitte, I said, 'No more gray!'"

"I started to dress in a patchwork of bright colors. I wanted to show that I'm happy!" she says. "I'm not afraid. I continue to travel everywhere as a transgender woman. I feel powerful and safe."

"There is nothing queerer than nature." This was the theme of Brigitte's TED talk in 2018, which has been viewed almost 100,000 times. "It's time to reject homogeneity and make room for a real diversity, for the diversity that is represented by the interactions between all the people," she says. "It's time to build a version more joyful, more fun and most beautiful of nature."

In her TED talk Brigitte explains that "sometimes environmental policies are created for the conservation of green without really understanding that what is happening in the world is a constant arrangement and change of the species that are interacting and are actively evolving. Actually, that exercise of simplification of the world, of detaching from the world, has led us to create a perspective tremendously homogeneous of it. A perspective in which diversity and gender diversity, and sexual diversity, are no longer important. A world in which relationships between the species and between us and nature change substantially in meaning. That's why I think it's time to rejoin and rescue sexual and gender diversity in our visions of nature."

When she talks to audiences, Brigitte stresses the importance of having hope for the future for all living beings. "I have faith in this evolving world. We have the capacity to overcome this environmental crisis. We can regenerate and restore life."

And if you bring up Colombian coffee with Brigitte, she'll enthusiastically tell you how to grow coffee and why Colombian coffee tastes so incredible. "That's one of my favorite subjects," she says. "Half a million families here depend on coffee production for their daily income."

She emphasizes how connected ecology is to growing coffee and to sustaining life in the forest. "Everybody can help with ecological restoration," she says.

Follow Brigitte Baptiste Online

Twitter: @Brigittelgb

Instagram: @BrigitteLGB

Trailblazers:

Rachel Levine, President Biden's assistant secretary for health, is the highest-ranking openly transgender person ever to serve in the federal government. She's the first openly transgender person ever confirmed by the Senate.

Sarah McBride, a Democratic LGBTQ activist, was the first transgender person of any political party to address a national convention, when she spoke at the 2016 Democratic National Convention (DNC). The crowd cheered "We love you, Sarah!"

Since she was 13 years old, Sarah had been fascinated by Barack Obama, who was then an Illinois state senator. She even reconstructed the DNC stage in her bedroom and practiced reciting Obama's keynote address and his other speeches.

Sarah went on to win the Delaware state senate race in 2020, and in so doing has become the first openly transgender state senator and the country's highest-ranking transgender official. "I hope tonight shows an LGBTQ kid that our democracy is big enough for them, too," Sarah tweeted after winning her election.

At age 26, **Taylor Small** became Vermont's first trans-gender legislator in history in 2020. On her platform, Taylor was very vocal about climate change and the need for Vermont to transition to clean energy sources. She says it's all about funding, and the finances we need to switch to renewable energy.

In January 2022, **Andrea Jenkins** became the first openly trans city council president in the United States. "We will reimagine, reconcile and repair the harms of the past," Jenkins said the night she won the election as Minneapolis City Council President, reading from a poem she had written. "We are stronger than we know. . . . We will heal. We will heal. We will heal."

9

Jeanette Davis:
Just Keep Swimming

Jeanette Davis headed off to Hampton University in Virginia with a settled plan. She planned to sign up for the premed program and tread the long path to become a medical doctor. "I thought, *If you love science, then you go to medical school.*"

But before classes started, she happened to walk past the school's marine science department. Her curiosity piqued, she went inside. The department chair introduced himself and shared the curriculum with her.

It was a life-changing moment. "I realized that I'm not a medical doctor!" Jeanette says.

She half-jokes that she signed up to take every "ology" class offered. (The suffix *-ology* refers to "the study of" a particular subject.) Biology. Zoology. Microbiology. Geology. Jeanette can't get enough.

Marine science encompasses so many different sciences under one umbrella. "Studying the ocean is actually studying the combination of so many sciences." As a kid, Jeanette loved to explore everything—plants, beehives, life on the beach—so marine science is a perfect fit for her.

A Day in the Life of a Marine Scientist

Even after decades of discoveries, humans have explored only a small percentage of the ocean. Marine scientists studying the deep are like pioneers charting a new frontier. Each year, new marine species are discovered and described. Many of these new species live in the deep sea.

Humans are drawn to the sea because it makes us curious, but we also depend on it for food and other resources, as well as transportation. The ocean helps make life on Planet Earth possible. It absorbs heat from the sun and moves this heat around, keeping temperatures on land from becoming too extreme. The tiny marine plants that live in the ocean create oxygen that humans and other land animals breathe. Even though humans can visit the underwater world, we haven't spent enough time there to know all of its secrets.

In 1979, Sylvia Earle, an American marine scientist and explorer, took a big step for underwater exploration. Sylvia walked untethered on the seafloor at 1,250 feet (381 m), a lower depth than any other human, in a device called a JIM suit that protected her from the extreme pressure. She explored for two and a half hours.

This sidebar is excerpted from *Marine Science for Kids: Exploring and Protecting Our Watery World*, by Josh and Bethanie Hestermann, Chicago Review Press, 2017.

The next summer, Jeanette got an internship with a group called Multicultural Students at Sea Together. She and 10 other students boarded a 53-foot (16.2-m) sailboat that changed the course of her life.

Jeanette and the crew spent one month sailing around Chesapeake Bay. "I immersed myself," she says, explaining that the boat stopped at research institutes along the bay, so students could dig deeper and learn.

Jeanette earned her bachelor's degree in marine and environmental science and set her sights on getting her PhD from the University of Maryland, one of the schools where she'd made a research stop during that month on the sailboat.

She heard a lecture about how you can find and discover medicines that exist in the sea. This is what led to her research in marine drugs and earning her doctorate in marine microbiology, bioinformatics, and marine ecology. She wrote her dissertation on herbivorous mollusks (sacoglossans), or "solar-powered sea slugs." These slugs shed their bodies, including the whole heart, and are able to regenerate a new body!

Jeanette now gets to do what she has always loved. "I grew up loving science and I loved being outdoors," she says. "But I never articulated that I wanted to be a scientist because I didn't know that was something you could do."

Jeanette says that part of getting her PhD—and becoming a good scientist—is learning how to accept failure and do things over and over and over again until you get it.

This is also how Jeanette got curious about implementing what's called environmental DNA (eDNA) both to research drugs and also to detect invasive species. The same way that someone might leave behind hair or blood at a crime scene, animals in the sea are constantly shedding their scales or skin.

For her current (water pun intended!) work, she says, "I use these tools and other scientific skills for decision making and management of ocean resources in government. . . . These eDNA tools are especially important with climate change because they allow us to track marine biota in an ever-changing environment." Some days, she goes to sea to find and examine water samples. Other days, she's in her office, writing up plans, researching policy, or speaking with members of Congress about the importance of investing in scientific tools for ocean science.

"I'm CSI for the marine environment," says Jeanette, refer-ring to *CSI: Crime Scene Investigation*, a TV drama about a team of forensic investigators trained to solve criminal cases by scouring the scene.

As a marine microbiologist, she focuses "on the things you can't see without a microscope."

Jeanette also encourages everyone around her to ask questions. "It's important to ask about your quality of air, your water, and your food. It's important to hold external people accountable."

As a Black woman in marine science, Jeanette has also experienced racism. "You're too ambitious" or "Aim a little lower" or "Just because you have a PhD doesn't mean you can . . ." are just a few of the stifling criticisms she's confronted.

The gender and race gap in STEM (science, technology, engineering, and mathematics) still persists around the world. But Jeanette has a message of resilience: "Through these experiences I've learned brilliance and joy is the best response. It's time to build our own equity in marine science!"

"I want equality, equity, and the freedom to do science without someone questioning my credentials," Jeanette says.

You might remember New York City's birdwatching confrontation in 2020 when a White woman walking her dog harassed Christian Cooper, a Black birdwatcher, in a section of Central Park known as the Ramble.

Following this incitement, Black birders created #BlackBirdersWeek to celebrate Black birders and their right to belong and feel in nature. Since then, many campaigns have surfaced to amplify and appreciate Black academics, scientists, and naturalists, such as #BlackInNature.

Jeanette and three other Black female shark researchers kept the momentum going by cofounding Black in Marine Science, a premier organization established to celebrate Black marine scientists, spread environmental awareness, and inspire the next generation of scientific thought leaders. Their mission is "to be seen and take up space in a discipline which has been largely inaccessible for women like us. We strive to be positive role models for the next generation. We seek to promote diversity and inclusion in shark science and encourage women of color to push through barriers and contribute knowledge in marine science."

"We are working to make sure young people know what it's like to work in this field," Jeanette says. "It's not just about being Black. We're scientists who happen to be Black."

Jeanette has worked with members of Congress to highlight the need for those who make decisions about ocean-dependent communities to represent the needs of diverse communities, especially on topics such as climate change.

Fun fact: Jeanette was a consultant on *Black Panther: Wakanda Forever* (2022), a Marvel movie about protecting the land under the sea.

As a Black marine scientist, Jeanette is proud to be a role model in the lives of her 14 nieces and nephews. "Science is everywhere, and science is for everyone," she tells them. "This is my motto."

This is also why Jeanette decided to write a book in 2020 called *Science Is Everywhere: Science Is for Everyone*. She aims to show that science doesn't just happen in a lab. She also wants to show young readers how diverse science is.

In 2022 she followed up with another book, *Jada's Journey Under the Sea*, to introduce young readers to all the fun and innovative ways they can learn about the ocean environment and how to protect it. Over the years Jeanette has searched for kids' books that highlight Black scientists in their fields, and the selection is bleak. After all, curiosity as a kid is part of what led Jeanette to study science, and she is determined to share this experience with young readers.

Follow Jeanette Davis Online

Website: https://drjeanettedavis.com/

Twitter: @DrOcean24

Instagram: Dr_Ocean24

Follow Black in Marine Science Online

Website: https://www.blackinmarinescience.org/

Twitter: @BlackinMarSci

Instagram: @Blackinmarinescience

Trailblazer: Carlee Jackson

When Carlee Jackson was a five-year-old kid in Detroit, Michigan, her mom took her to a book fair, where a book about sharks caught her eye.

"The cover had a close-up picture of a shark, and it drew me in," remembers Carlee. "After begging my mom to buy the book for me, I read it and was obsessed. I found sharks to be the coolest animals, and I realized how misunderstood they were. From that moment on, sharks were my favorite animal, and I knew I wanted to work with them some day."

Carlee points to this moment as leading her to study marine biology in college and becoming a shark researcher. After getting a bachelor's of science in biology from Florida Atlantic University, she completed a master's in marine biology at Nova Southeastern University.

As part of her master's research, she got to travel to Caye Caulker, Belize, to study the effects of provisioning (feeding) tourism on nurse sharks. Nurse sharks are slow-moving bottom-dwellers that can grow up to 14 feet (4.3 m). They have very strong jaws filled with thousands of tiny serrated teeth. They eat fish, shrimp, and squid.

"Studying how this human activity affects nurse sharks is essential in conservation and management of this species, as their numbers are decreasing," Carlee says. "Specifically, I wanted to know how it was affecting their swimming behavior and how attracted they were to the feeding site."

She conducted surveys with the sharks at a feeding site by filming them with GoPros. "I found that the nurse sharks were modifying their natural behavior in order to gain access to a valuable resource: food."

This project was an example of how humans have unfavorably affected species' habitats and behavior in the world. After graduating, Carlee got a job as a sea turtle research associate for the New College of Florida, where she's contracted to explore marine conservation at the Walt Disney Company.

In June 2020, during the pandemic, thanks to #BlackInNature—which was created as part of #BlackBirdersWeek—Black women scientists began to find each other online.

This is how Carlee connected with Jasmin Graham (featured in the following sidebar), Jaida Elcock, and Amani Webber-Schultz, all successful Black women working in the field of shark science.

Carlee posted pictures of herself doing fieldwork with sharks and sea turtles. "Jasmin commented on my post expressing how excited she was to see a fellow Black woman in shark science. I was floored and couldn't believe she was a shark scientist too! Soon after, Jaida and Amani were in my comments saying they were shark scientists, and we jokingly suggested starting a club."

They organized a Zoom call. "We talked about how much it meant to us to find each other, and how difficult it was to navigate this field as a Black woman," Carlee says. "We decided we didn't want anyone else to feel alone like we did, so we created a space for women of color in shark sciences with the goal of breaking down systemic barriers preventing people of color from entering this field."

They had a lot in common. While studying and working in marine biology, they were often the only Black females in class or on-site. They'd all experienced firsthand how challenging it can be to stick it out in a field where there's so little diversity or support.

"I went my entire career thinking I was the only Black woman in the field of shark science," Carlee adds. "Meeting three other Black women in the same field was mind-blowing to me."

Together, these four women founded Minorities in Shark Sciences (MISS), with Jasmin as CEO, Jaida as director of public relations, Amani as CFO, and Carlee as director of communications. "It's been life changing as we are doing things in this field that had never been done before," says Carlee.

This is how MISS was conceived. "None of us truly understood how much we had been craving such a community until we found it," say the four founders. Thanks to these four scientists, women of color who are interested in studying sharks now have a space to feel welcome and supported.

If she could tell her younger self anything, Carlee would say, "Every time you feel like a failure or get discouraged, know that you end up accomplishing one of your biggest dreams."

Trailblazer: Jasmin Graham

It's spring, which means it's sawfish season in the Atlantic Ocean, so researcher Jasmin Graham is out on a boat surveying endangered animals. Sawfish are a kind of ray, and they are Jasmin's specialty.

"They're listed as endangered in the United States, so legally we have to protect them," says Jasmin, a marine biologist, environmental educator, and social justice activist. She's also the CEO and president of Minorities in Shark Sciences (MISS).

Monitoring the movement of sawfish might be a window into the climate crisis. Jasmin explains that the sawfish has lost much of its natural habitat in the Florida mangroves.

"This has a lot to do with the warming waters, but it also has to do with how we are modifying the coastline," Jasmin says. "So, protecting these areas is a super-big, important step. It means that we're not only protecting this region for sawfish, but also all of the other animals."

The extended nose of the sawfish actually looks like a saw, and they can grow to be 17 feet (5.2 m) long. Jasmin says they can look intimidating if you look at them from the top down, but from the bottom they have cute, gray mouths that kind of look like they're smiling.

Growing up, Jasmin's dad often took the family out fishing. "My dad's side of the family is from Myrtle Beach, South Carolina, so it's all coastal seafood for us," she says. "It's practically built into the fabric of our DNA as a family."

Jasmin was precociously curious about the ocean. She wanted to swim! "I wanted to get into the water, and my family would say, 'Girl, what are you doing?'" she laughs.

Jasmin was a sophomore in high school the first time she'd heard about marine biology. "I thought, *Wait, people pay you to do this? This is awesome!*"

Her family, however, wasn't so sure. They were supportive, but they didn't know anyone who made a living in marine science. "They encouraged me to major in biology." They figured that if marine science didn't work out, Jasmin could be a doctor.

"A doctor, a lawyer, or an engineer. Those are the jobs that smart people have if you do well in school. That's understandable," she says, thoughtful about where her family was coming from.

Jasmin figured that she'd become a veterinarian, because at least she'd get to work with animals. "Then I figured out that veterinarian school is really hard to get into and really expensive," she says. "And then I thought, *Why the heck am I trying to put a square peg into a round hole? I'm just going to do what I wanted to do in the first place!*"

She switched her degree to marine biology: "And that's how I got here." Jasmin adds that she had never met a Black woman scientist in person until she was in her early 20s.

"When you picture a shark scientist, what do you see?" asks Jasmin. "When you watch Shark Week, what do you see? Do you see someone who looks like me? I am a Black woman, and I am a shark scientist, and a darn good one at that."

Today in the Tampa Bay region of Florida, Jasmin's focus is on shark research and conservation. She explains how mangroves provide protection from storms on the coast, and also act as "nurseries" for wildlife to breed. Mangroves are incredible trees that are native to Florida. They thrive in salty water because they are able to get freshwater from saltwater by secreting excess salt through their leaves!

Unfortunately, humans have destroyed mangrove habitat by dredging, filling, water pollution, and development. When mangrove forests are cleared, massive amounts of carbon dioxide are released into the atmosphere, adding to climate change.

Sawfish live in mangroves, Jasmin explains. "So if you protect mangroves because you are trying to save this critically endangered species, you are also protecting everything else that [benefits from] mangroves."

Jasmin loves to talk about her favorite shark, the bonnethead. They're the smallest of the 10 hammerhead shark species.

The World Wildlife Fund awarded Jasmin its Conservation Leadership Award in 2021 "to give the next generation of conservation leaders access to a global platform and experts."

Jasmin is currently the project coordinator at Marine Science Laboratory Alliance Center of Excellence, an organization that recruits, supports, and retains minority students in marine science.

Jasmin is also planning the activities for the first annual free summer camp that MISS is hosting for teens to introduce them to the world of marine science. "I'm going to throw them in the deep end with shark dissection!" she laughs. "It's going to be fun."

Jasmin adds, "I love it when girls of color come up to me and say, 'I want to do what you do!' Having these conversations is really impactful!"

Trailblazer: Leslie Townsell

"Water has always been a safe space for me," says marine scientist Leslie Townsell, who's currently a graduate student at the University of Georgia, where her research explores the impacts of climate change on oyster aquaculture along the coast.

Leslie always thought she'd become a pediatrician. "But when I was in undergrad pursuing a biology degree with a premed concentration, I was speaking with my adviser, and I realized I didn't have a passion for medicine."

After enrolling in an independent research course about limnology—the study of inland aquatic ecosystems, such as lakes, ponds, rivers, wetlands, and more—Leslie says, "I realized marine biology was my life's calling!"

Her goal is to increase the sustainability of Georgia's coastal fisheries and promote healthy coastal ecosystems. While at the University of Georgia, Leslie noticed the lack of Black scientists. This is how she connected to women like marine microbiologist Jeanette Davis (featured in this book) to create Black in Marine Science, a nonprofit that promotes and amplifies the voices of Black marine scientists.

Founded by Tiara Moore—a postdoc scholar at the University of Washington and the Nature Conservancy in Washington—Black in Marine Science (BIMS) increases the visibility of Black marine scientists.

"On my life's highlight reel, Black in Marine Science holds the top spot," says Leslie. "Helping to start BIMS was a huge turning point in my life. Before BIMS I felt so isolated and alone. Now there is a community that I can look up to and rely on and just be myself with no matter what."

10

Nikki Roach:
A Day in the Life of
a Conservation Biologist

As a teen growing up in Oakland, California, the idea of leaving her house sometimes made Nikki Roach sick to her stomach. Whether it was a short walk to the grocery store or a slumber party with her friends, Nikki's heart pounded, and her insides cramped up. Her thoughts spiraled as she imagined leaving the confines of her safety net.

What if she panicked? And then what? Who would help her?

"My fear is anxiety itself," Nikki says, explaining that one of her biggest fears is being all alone during a panic attack and having no one to help her.

"I can't pinpoint any one incident triggering my anxiety. It's been this way my entire life." Nikki says that she used to walk around looking for the first place to exit. She remembers being hypervigilant of her surroundings, always looking for a way out if she got too anxious.

Even so, Nikki says that by the time she was in high school, "I had vivid dreams of traveling and living abroad for long periods of time. But there was always that nagging thought in my head. Could I do it?"

When it was time to go to college, Nikki decided to attend University of California, Davis, which was just an hour away from home. This is where she earned a bachelor's degree in conservation biology.

She worked for both the US Fish and Wildlife Service and US Geological Survey and then moved all the way across the country to study for her master's degree at Clemson University in South Carolina, in the Department of Forestry and Environmental Conservation. Nikki spent summers in Bennett's Point—which she describes as "a small, isolated shrimping town"—to do her fieldwork.

So much was new and different for her, like her fellow students who wore T-shirts that read, HUNTIN' BUCKS, DRIVIN' TRUCKS. THAT'S HOW I ROLL. Bennett's Point is a town that relies heavily on shrimping. This is how people here feed their families.

Nikki loved seeing the marsh pulse with life and seeing how intertwined wildlife and humans are. She dove right into her work in the field, settling into a rhythm where she felt most at peace—in nature. She describes herself as someone who will "geek out over anything alive—lizards, frogs, birds, trees, crabs, cattle, stray dogs and cats. Pretty much if it's moving, it's cool."

She studied marsh birds to learn how vulnerable they are to rising sea levels. Specifically, she followed the endangered eastern black rails that live in the dense marshes in Bennett's Point.

"Marsh birds are extremely secretive and are often not seen but heard," Nikki says, explaining why she used something called "auditory surveys" to collect data. "Yes, we basically play bird calls and then listen for a response. We couple this information with local and landscape environmental variables that may affect marsh bird occurrence throughout South Carolina."

The goal was to communicate her findings to land managers and federal and state employees in conservation planning efforts. On weekends, Nikki was told that she could take a boat out to conduct her surveys. She'd never driven a boat before, but after a brief lesson, someone put the keys to the boat in her hands. Nikki named it "the Big Sexy."

"I crashed onto a sandbar the first time I ever took the boat out alone," she says, relieved there was no damage! Nikki challenged herself to say *yes* to new experiences. Like going to oyster roasts with local shrimpers and plantation managers, and even jumping off a bridge into alligator-infested waters. "Pushing myself beyond my own anxieties into the realm of the unknown opened so many doors."

She applied to a PhD program and was so excited to get her acceptance letter, but when she started to pack her bags, her anxiety crept back in. Nikki had been accepted to a PhD program at Texas A&M University in its applied biodiversity science program in College Station.

College Station is a historically conservative university town in central Texas. The nearest big cities, Austin and Houston, are about 100 miles (160 km) away. Texas A&M is home to the George H.W. Bush Presidential Library and Museum. Football reigns. There are no cheerleaders at the football games. Instead, there are "yell leaders," a tribute to the school's traditions as a senior military college.

"I quickly became depressed," Nikki reflects about starting school. "I had no friends there and I was consumed with anxiety, I couldn't eat or sleep."

Still, Nikki plowed through her studies, knowing that her research would take her back into the field outdoors. "There was immense pressure to perform in graduate school, to get good grades, to raise money for my PhD research, and to write a research proposal on top of managing other tasks," she says.

"I have anxiety *and* I have a desire to follow through and challenge myself, so the anxiety makes things extra challenging because I am already nervous about it," Nikki says. "Like I might say, 'Oh, I'll never do these things.' . . . And then I do them. When I started my PhD, I told myself that there were three things I absolutely would not do: work at night, alone, in the jungle."

Well, in the end, that's exactly what Nikki did: she moved to Sierra Nevada de Santa Marta, the world's tallest coastal tropical mountain range in the world! This is where Nikki landed in the jungle to work at night to research amphibians and varying levels of land use, including coffee farms.

How Your Blended Iced Coffee Is Connected to Climate Change

Colombian coffee farmers are paying the price for climate change, and small farms are being hit the hardest. The mountain region here, where coffee is grown, has been warming by 0.3 degrees Celsius (0.5 degrees Fahrenheit) every decade. Coffee trees are very sensitive to any changes in weather, which makes it challenging to sustain a coffee farm with climate change.

Coffee farmers often live on less than two dollars a day. In order to make a living, some farmers have replaced their coffee trees with higher-value crops like avocado or coca leaf, which is used to make cocaine. Colombia's leading agricultural breadwinner is cocaine. Coffee comes in second.

Sierra Nevada de Santa Marta is in one of the world's most unique protected area for threatened species, such as endangered harlequin frogs and the vivid Santa Marta parakeet. Here, Nikki managed a team of four people to research threatened amphibian communities on local coffee farms. "The work was very physically demanding," she says, describing her days rising with the sun, "whether I like it or not."

After her early morning coffee, Nikki ate breakfast and prepared to hike out to either the coffee field or the forest with her two field assistants, Jeferson "Jef" Villalba and José Perez-Gonzalez.

"This is the most difficult part of the day," she says about having to use a "machete to carve our way through dense forest, slipping and sliding on mud and tree roots while avoiding falling rocks."

Part of Nikki's job was to place something called "transects" in the field. "Transects are 30-meter-long designated paths that we would walk searching for amphibians," Nikki notes. "Once we found an amphibian, we would take identify the species and sex if possible and take morphological [physical] measurements."

After a big lunch back at camp before the afternoon rains (aka *aguaceros*), Nikki would rest or read back in her tent. One season, she reread all the Harry Potter books during her afternoon downtime. "Harry Potter was a form of comfort to me when I was so far removed into another world," she says. "It helped me relax while in the field."

Then it was back to the field, after making sure that her crew had enough batteries to last them five hours during the night. "As night falls, the forest transforms from difficult terrain to an almost-unrecognizable death trap," she says. "We slip and slide our way through dense coffee plants—grabbing ahold to branches so we don't fall down the 45-degree slope—or I go down a hill, almost on my butt, and hop rocks within the streams to get to the first flag we placed 'close by' earlier in the day."

Of course, Nikki often caught more than frogs. "Ants, scorpions, mosquitoes, snakes, and huge spiders all appear along our transects," she recalls. "Can I just take a minute to say how much I *hate* biting insects? . . . Some nights we find up to 12 species of frogs, while others we are lucky to find one frog, period."

"Did I mention all of this happens in Spanish?"

She's grateful that she's never alone in the field thanks to her Spanish-speaking Colombian research assistants. "I used to be very scared of night work. You can't see very far, and you're wearing a headlamp. I used to fall a lot." Some nights, she didn't return to her campsite until midnight, after walking for hours from sundown until the next morning. "One night we were out until 2:00 AM," she recalls.

The next morning, as the sun hit the side of her tent, it was time to do it all over again.

Nikki posted a photo of herself captioned "A Day in the Field" and wrote, "To note: I bathe minimally, because it is already cold on the mountain and there is no warm water, this means maybe one to three showers every 10 days or so. . . . I also rarely change my clothes and wear the same fit basically every day. Pretty much I think I probably smell and look awesome."

She recalls how she always seemed to get her period right when she was headed out on a monthly trek into the jungle, where she managed multiple projects and crews as "the only *gringa* in town!"

Nikki spent three years working in Colombia. In total, she studied 19 species of the amphibian community to see how vulnerable they are to both land use and climate change.

"I also interviewed coffee farmers to better understand their perceptions and land use practices as they relate to biodiversity conservation. From 2019–2020 I led a project called Filters for Frogs, where we examined the quality of coffee wastewater to better understand the impact coffee plantations have on the surrounding amphibian habitat."

Nikki created the hashtag #FilterForFrogs on Twitter owing to the lack of frogs on coffee farms. She was determined to find out where the frogs were! "Sixteen of the 19 species I worked with were endemic—or only found in the Sierra Nevada de Santa Marta."

"I was curious about the contamination between the coffee farms and the streams with wastewater from coffee runoff and pesticides." She studied the watersheds, which are the land that drains into the streams and rivers. Watersheds are important not only for frogs but also for mammals and humans.

Every week, Nikki ventured farther into the jungle to research. "There was a lot of self-talk to remind myself, *OK,*

Nikki, you're two days from the closest town, but nothing is going to happen to you or your crew."

What Does a Conservation Biologist Do?

Conservation biologists are scientists who study the Earth's biodiversity with the goal of protecting ecosystems, which are the habitats of both plant and animal species. If you're thinking about studying conservation biology, you probably like to get to "into the weeds" and interact with the world around you.

You will probably focus on the climate, researching environmental trends and solutions to restore and maintain healthy ecosystems. You might collaborate and support government agencies, landowners, and the public. If you get a degree in conservation biology, you might work as a wildlife or land trust biologist, researcher, natural resources manager, or more!

One day, when Nikki had gone to the capital city of Bogotá to get her visa, she didn't feel well. "But I'd often felt sick because of the high altitude. I thought it was gas, but I couldn't stop throwing up."

A friend took her to a public hospital, where she spent 16 hours, "hunched between two Colombian old men, throwing up in a plastic bag. . . . I had appendicitis."

"My mom flew down that night and came to meet me in the hospital. I was laughing and crying because I couldn't believe it," she mentions. "I didn't have health insurance in the US, so I was lucky that everything happened there [because] Colombia has socialized health insurance. I was really lucky in that sense."

At the end of her PhD, Nikki was recognized as outstanding PhD student of the year for her department. "Colombia is a magical place," she says. "I absolutely adore Santa Marta, the people, the warm air, and mountain mist. I think it is one of the most beautiful places in the world. I feel incredibly fortunate to have spent so much time there."

By the time Nikki headed back to the United States in March 2020, the COVID-19 pandemic was in full force all over the world. Nikki gave a shout-out on social media to "be responsible and stay at home to protect each other. So please do your part."

Nikki moved back into her childhood bedroom in her parents' house, where she spent lots of time with their dog, Lola. She went camping and to the beach, and she also dated a Colombian guy whom she'd met online.

Today, Nikki sums up her anxiety as "a constant battle" to overcome her fears about the unknown. Over the years, Nikki has found tools to help talk herself down from what she calls her "bouts of crippling anxiety," including reaching out to friends, going to therapy, dancing, hiking, meditating, doing yoga, and reading.

Most recently, she devoured the novel *Homegoing* by Yaa Gyasi in a few days before heading off to the International

Union for Conservation of Nature World Conservation Congress in Marseille, France, along with 4,000 other participants. No doubt, Nikki will connect with some kind, compassionate scientists along the way, breathe through her fears, and explore some exciting new paths.

Follow Nikki Roach Online

Website: http://nroach.weebly.com/

Twitter: @niksroach

Part III
Take a Stand for Justice

Amy Cardinal Christianson:
Burning Good Fires

Amy Cardinal Christianson, a member of the Métis Nation, looks out to a clearing encircled by spruce trees in northern Alberta, Canada, as she holds her daughter's hand. Several of Amy's fire research colleagues from California and Australia are gathered around, listening to Amy speak as smoke rises in the near distance and turns the sky hazy.

"For me, fire was a part of life, because I grew up in a forest that needed fire," Amy says, adding that "lots of my extended family are involved in firefighting, including my husband, who's a wildland firefighter." Amy is pregnant with her second daughter as she speaks calmly to her colleagues from her spot in the sunlit grassy field.

Amy works for the Canadian Forest Service as a fire research scientist, and she's explaining to the group how Indigenous families like hers have burned fires here for thousands of years to take care of the land.

Indigenous peoples raised generations of families here, with fire as an integral part of their lives. That is, until white colonizers settled here and began to exclude and suppress fires. "Fire is part of the environment, and if used properly it can be really good," Amy explains.

She describes what a "good fire" is: it's a fire that you light intentionally when the conditions are right. A blaze actually helps the ecosystems by keeping the forest healthy.

Like water and sunlight, fire is vital to keep ecosystems thriving. Forests have been resilient for thousands of years, but colonizers squashed the traditional practices that kept them flourishing.

In the Western world, people often see fire as a threat. But burning intentional fires is part of a holistic care for the land. This means that fire is a way to clear out dead litter on forest floors and allow nutrients to return to the soil, so new plants can grow and thrive.

One of Amy's missions is to educate people about good fires. She even started the *Good Fire* podcast to have conversations with other Indigenous peoples about their experiences. "We're not experts, we're knowledge holders, or whatever you'd like to call us, so we get a lot of similar questions," Amy says. "So now, with the podcast, people can get an overview about good fire. A podcast is a great medium for being able to communicate with people."

When Amy was young, she was always very interested in extreme weather events, like tornadoes and earthquakes. In college she first majored in atmospheric sciences but then decided to study geology. She went on to get her masters in New Zealand in volcanic hazard management.

"I was supposed to do physical risk mapping on a volcano," Amy says. "But then I found out that I was way more interested in the human aspect of risk. So, I ended up shifting my focus to humans, and doing my PhD in hazard management and fire science." Amy went on to write a couple of books, including *First Nations Wildfire Evacuations: A Guide for Communities and External Agencies* and *Blazing the Trail: Celebrating Indigenous Fire Stewardship.*

The gist of Amy's message is "Don't fear fire." Along with the environmental benefits of burning intentional fires, there's also a cultural side for Indigenous people. Fires are empowering. They're a way to connect to the land, to one's ancestors, and to the health of a community.

How Good Fire Can Help Our Forests

Alejandra Borunda, environment writer for *National Geographic,* says she became a "fire writer" on the job as fires burned across the American West.

"Fire season is interminable here," Alejandra says, explaining that fires have been burning perpetually on the West Coast. "There is no more fire season. Fire season is year round."

The more that Alejandra, who's based in Southern California, researches and writes about fires for *National Geographic*, the more she realizes that "explaining the relationship between climate change and fire is not the whole story at all!" Here's what Alejandra realized: wildfire is inevitable. In other words, prescribed burning—meaning "good fires," or fires that are carefully and intentionally set—can actually help manage the risks of wildfires.

In one story, Alejandra describes how fire is a natural part of the life cycle of a forest. Yes, this might seem counterintuitive, but you may be surprised to learn that many species of trees in the western United States actually need fire to survive. For example, the seeds of the giant sequoia need the intense heat of fire to release from their cones and germinate.

"This fire problem is not just because of climate change," Alejandra says, explaining that before white settlers came to the United States, an estimated 4.5 million acres of forest burned every year, set either by lightning or Indigenous communities, who used fire to take care of the land.

Prescribed burns—planned and controlled fires—are effective, Alejandra says.

Fortunately, Alejandra says that fire and policy experts are "recognizing that the way we've been doing things is not working. . . . Just fighting the fires as they come is not enough. And it's not safe."

"I think the difficulty with Indigenous fire is that it's not really something you can just incorporate or blend into kind of an existing agency fire program, unless you hire a bunch of Indigenous peoples," Amy says. "There's such a lack of understanding of Indigenous peoples and their relationship to fire."

Fire management looks to Amy because she has interviewed and worked with so many people who've experienced massive wildfires and evacuations. "I'm really privileged in my job because I get to go around and meet other Indigenous peoples from other countries who've experienced similar issues and work with a bunch of different Elders and fire keepers."

"Indigenous peoples have always been adaptive," Amy says. "When colonizers came, it was probably one of the biggest adaptation events ever. We had to go from our way of life to totally learning another. Most of those Nations are still here, like my Nation, and we're still fighting. It's the same with climate change.

"There's still a lot of existing knowledge, and there's Indigenous knowledge that's developed every day from this close relationship with the land. Indigenous peoples have that inherent right to be able to steward our territories."

Follow Amy Cardinal Christianson Online

Twitter: @ChristiansonAmy

Trailblazer: Debra Utacia Krol

"Do you know those sad stories where people are in tears when they're done?" asks Debra Utacia Krol, Indigenous affairs reporter at the *Arizona Republic*.

Debra—an enrolled member of the Xolon (also known as Jolon) Salinan tribe from the Central California coastal ranges—is referring to the stories that some journalists write about Indigenous people along the lines of "Oh, poor me, the salmon are going away" or "Oh, poor me, the abalone are going away." Well, Debra says we've had enough of those sad stories.

What we need are stories of resilience. The fact is, Indigenous communities are the most resilient in the world. Debra is an award-winning journalist who writes about Native issues and environmental issues. "My beat is Indians," she says.

For example, in one of Debra's award-winning features, she infuses history into the story, a history that most Americans have not learned. When naturalist John Muir first got to Yosemite Valley, he wrote that he had found "nature's landscape garden." "What Muir didn't recognize was that the lush valley resulted not from the hand of Mother Nature but from human hands as Indigenous peoples carefully trimmed plants to make them grow straight, kept watersheds pristine and periodically burned the land to clear dead material and stimulate fresh green growth," Debra writes.

Debra describes how Europeans "herded Native peoples off most of their ancestral lands and confined them to first the missions, then to tiny plots of land known as rancherias."

When Native peoples tried to practice cultural burns, colonists either killed or jailed them. "Federal land policies that supported fire suppression, commercial agriculture, and forestry replaced Indigenous land management," in Debra's words.

Indigenous communities often grapple with issues of inaccurate information and incomplete stories. One of Debra's missions is to educate people about tribal perspectives that are often ignored or dismissed.

"I would like to see a bit more about what tribes are doing to address the abalone and salmon issues, because they are real issues," Debra says, explaining that the media often covers these issues in ways that are stereotypical. One example she points out is how salmon are dying "precipitously but nobody seems to be writing about what the salmon tribes are doing to address it, or what they are advocating for other governments to do, or to partner with them."

In Northern California, Debra covers the ongoing drought and how catastrophic it is for salmon in this region. "At least two tribes, the Yurok and the Karuk, have declared states of emergency, hoping to gain attention to the very real possibility that at least one key salmon species will soon go extinct," Debra writes. "Indigenous peoples across the globe, confronting the realities of climate change from the front lines, have long warned of these and other effects of a rapidly heating world."

She says it's time for people—scientists, policymakers, journalists, and more—to acknowledge "the commonalities between their own disciplines and Indigenous sciences, including traditional ecological knowledge, or TEK."

TEK means "a tribal community's accumulated knowledge of its lands, ecologies, biodiversity, and material culture." In other words, Indigenous communities have thousands of years of knowledge about the environment that they've acquired through direct contact with the land.

12

Anna Jane Joyner: Flipping the Script on Climate

During her sophomore year of college, Anna Jane Joyner got the chance to study abroad in New Zealand. During a break from school, she and her best friend were scrolling through the website FindACrew.com—"which I don't advise doing," Anna Jane notes.

That's how these two friends found a captain who was looking for a crew to cross the Tasman Sea from Australia to New Zealand. After spending a month training with the captain, a retired American marine who'd sailed around the world, they set off on their voyage.

"The stars were insane and there was noctiluca, the shimmery stuff in the water that's also called bioluminescence. So, at night, it would feel like you were surrounded by stars up above you and below you," Anna Jane says. "There were dolphins everywhere. It was just a really magical, beautiful experience."

What's Below the Edge of Darkness?

"If you are ever lucky enough to dive deep into the ocean in a submersible, be sure to turn out the lights," says Edith (or "Edie") Widder, an expert in bioluminescence, biologist, and deep-sea explorer.

Bioluminescence is when a living being emits light through chemical reactions in its body. Bioluminescent organisms are common in the oceans but uncommon on land. Edie studies how and why there are so many creatures in the ocean that make light.

Edie dreamed about becoming a marine biologist, but after complications from a surgery in college, she went temporarily blind. Seeing shifting shadows fascinated her about the power of light.

The first time that Edie dove into the depths of the ocean, she had to wear a deep-diving suit called the Wasp, with a yellow body and bubble head. "That suit was not a comfortable ride!" Edie says. "It was sort of like being in a large, cold yo-yo as the tether attached to the surface ship yanked the suit up and down and the metal shell sucked body heat away into the numbing chill of the deep sea. But when I turned out the suit's headlights, the discomfort evaporated as I found myself surrounded by the greatest living light show on the planet.

Bioluminescence is everywhere in the oceans, and it's something that must be seen to be believed. That light show changed the course of my career."

From that day, Eddie was hooked. She had to know: Why is there so much light down there? Today Edie is the cofounder, CEO, and senior scientist at the Ocean Research & Conservation Association, a nonprofit organization where she is focusing her passion for saving the ocean into developing innovative technologies. Her memoir, *Below the Edge of Darkness*, published in 2021, was described by the *New York Times Book Review* as a "thrilling blend of hard science and high adventure."

But about a week into their trip, a big storm hit. "It was out of the blue. It hadn't even shown up on the radar, and it quickly got very scary." Anna Jane grabbed the sail when something called "the topping lift" broke.

"It could easily have thrown me out or killed me," she recalls. The captain told them to lock everything up and go underboard. "It was the first time in his 20 years of sailing that he had ever had to do that. So that's what we did."

They had no control of the boat as the rain pelted down. "I was sitting there hugging my teddy bear because I still had this teddy bear that my dad gave me. It was the most anxiety I've ever felt, and later I'd learn that what I was feeling was a panic attack."

The next day, they managed to surf their way to a little island called Lord Howe Island, otherwise known as "Just Paradise." "It was a near death experience," Anna Jane says. "We literally went from hell to heaven in like a 12-hour period."

"I called my dad and told him that I'd just gotten in a shipwreck and that I needed him to wire me some money. I told him that I loved him. He kept that voicemail for years."

But there was a catch. Her dad said that he'd continue to send her money to pay for her college tuition *only* if she went back to church.

Anna Jane's dad, Rick Joyner, is one of the most well-known men in the evangelical world. An evangelical preacher who presides over MorningStar Ministries, he oversees nearly 100 churches and ministries in dozens of countries.

"My dad is a conservative megachurch pastor," says Anna Jane, who comes from a line of proud Republicans. She even joined the Young Republicans club in high school.

But Anna Jane's semester abroad had opened her mind. She studied ecology and communications. When she told her dad that she planned to major in environmental studies, she was prepared for some pushback. But she did *not* expect her dad to stop paying for her school.

"He believed that I'd been brainwashed," she says. "So, he cut off my tuition."

"I was having a moral struggle," Rick Joyner says. "I was investing in having my daughter's mind corrupted. I can't pay to have this done to my daughter."

Anna Jane decided to stay in New Zealand. "I got a work visa. I loved the people there. My plan was to stay and make my life there."

Back at the University of North Carolina, Anna Jane found a more liberal church in North Carolina and graduated with a bachelor of arts in rhetoric and environmental studies. She wrote her thesis on biblical scriptures that address the moral reasons you should care about the climate. Her siblings followed her lead, distancing themselves from the evangelical church.

One year after graduating, Anna Jane cofounded a nonprofit organization called Renewal to mobilize students on faith-based campuses to rise up for the climate. Part of her mission was to help evangelical environmentalists find each other. She was the campaign director of Restoring Eden, a faith-based environmental nonprofit that led campaigns to shut down a coal-fired power plant in North Carolina.

During this time, Joel Bach and David Gelber were producing a Showtime documentary series called *Years of Living Dangerously*. They wanted to make an episode about climate change, so they approached Anna Jane and asked if they could film her—and her father. Anna Jane's goal was to persuade her father to change his mind about global warming.

Amazingly, her father agreed to be filmed as Anna Jane took him to meet several prominent climate change leaders. But her father refused to budge on his beliefs. "I tried to go into it as open as I possibly could," her dad says about being part of the Showtime documentary. "But I came out of it more of a skeptic than I came into it."

Anna Jane did not give up. For example, she wrote "An Open Letter to My Daddy Who Doesn't Accept Climate Change." "Daddy, I know you are someone who takes stewardship of creation as a moral mandate," Anna Janes wrote.

"I believe ignoring climate change is inconsistent with our faith. The risks are massive, and the science is clear. If we do nothing, our planet will face severe impacts, and billions of people will be hurt, most of whom contributed little or nothing to the problem. How is that just? How is that loving our neighbors?"

Jump ahead to 2020, when Donald Trump was up for reelection in the United States and the world was in lockdown during the COVID-19 pandemic.

Anna Jane's dad publicly urged Christians to mobilize to fight a war against left-wing activists. The media went to town with his message. "We're in time for war," he said. "We need to recognize that. We need to mobilize. We need to get ready."

"I'm solidly on the left, as are all my siblings," Anna Jane says. "So, when he does things like calling Democrats *evil*, it's very offensive and scary. If you are on the opposite side, it's like your dad is literally talking about waging a civil war against you, his own children."

To this day, Anna Jane's father refuses to accept that climate change is caused by humans. Yet the experience of making the film opened her eyes. She says that the screen has the power to reach people, and her father's resistance fuels her determination.

This is why, in 2020, Anna Jane decided to establish Good Energy, a nonprofit story consultancy that supports, in her words, "TV and film writers to weave climate themes into the fabric of popular shows and new films."

During the pandemic, Anna Jane was sheltered at home on the Gulf Coast of Alabama with her husband, her mother, her grandfather, and her two dogs and cat—Frannie, Remy, and Crockett—her fur babies.

Her mom grew up on the Gulf Coast of Alabama, and this is where Anna Jane spent her summers. "If there is a place in the world that is inseparable from my life, that is a physical and spiritual part of me, it is Perdido Beach in Alabama," Anna Jane says. "It is literally called 'the lost place,' *perdido*, because it's so tucked away."

She describes seeing dolphins every day in the Gulf of Mexico, and watching birds fly above the marsh. "One of the main reasons I wanted to live here is because as a climate activist, I knew that the Gulf Coast is incredibly vulnerable. I moved here with the purpose of honoring this place, witnessing it, and experiencing it. But I did not consider how truly stressful and traumatic living on the front lines of climate change actually is."

Anna Jane grew up in the Appalachian Mountains, where her dad took her and her siblings on Sunday hikes after church. "I hated it at first," she says. "We'd moved here from Charlotte, North Carolina, when I was 12, and I was a total mall rat. It was so rural, with cows blocking the road. My sister and I got freaked out by the wild turkeys."

In 2020 her father, an avid Trump supporter, was still calling for the next civil war, as Anna Jane campaigned for Joe Biden. "Hurricane Sally hit our home in September 2020," she says. "A lot of people don't even know this, but Sally was a really bad storm that wiped out a huge swath of the Gulf Coast across from Alabama to Florida. We still have tarps on our house from that storm. And there was just so much horrible news happening," she adds, referring to Trump, the rampant racism plaguing the country, and the isolation and deaths during the pandemic.

How Climate Change Makes Hurricanes Worse

"Climate change is making it more likely for hurricanes to behave in certain ways," according to James P. Kossin, a climate scientist with the National Oceanic and Atmospheric Administration.

Unusually high temperatures in the Gulf of Mexico are "like stepping on the accelerator," explains Brian Tang, an atmospheric scientist at the University at Albany in New York. According to the landmark United Nations climate report in 2021, warming from fossil fuel use and other human activities is likely behind the increase in the number of powerful hurricanes over the last four decades. Research shows that human greenhouse gas emissions have caused the ocean to warm faster in recent years than at any point since the end of the last ice age.

Anna Jane was living in what she calls "a state of high anxiety and stress." She couldn't sleep. "I went into a manic-depressive episode," she says. "My doctor is pretty convinced that it was a form of PTSD [post-traumatic stress disorder], intersecting with the fact that I am bipolar. The storm triggered this mental health breakdown."

It was the first time in her life that she'd experienced depression and manic episodes at the same time. "It was utterly terrifying. I just felt such a deep sense of pain, fear, and not being safe."

The hardest part, she says, was the fact that she couldn't focus on her climate work. She wasn't able to write or stay connected with other activists. "It is a very big part of who I am. And when I could no longer do it."

Her husband stepped in to help, along with her psychiatrist, and she was able to get the support she needed.

Yes, We're Anxious

In 2021 a group of researchers posted the results from the largest study of this kind ever done, in which they surveyed 10,000 young people (aged 16-25 years) in 10 countries.

They asked young people about their thoughts and feelings on climate change, and you probably won't be surprised that they're anxious. And they feel like their governments have betrayed them.

Nearly 60 percent of all young people said they felt "very worried" or "extremely worried." Many associated negative emotions with climate change—the most commonly chosen were "sad," "afraid," "anxious," "angry," and "powerless." Overall, 45 percent of participants said their feelings about climate change affected their daily lives.

Through her work running Good Energy, Anna Jane is "unlocking the power of TV and film to inspire courage in the face of climate change." Her goal? To save the planet through storytelling. "Hollywood can use its unparalleled influence over popular culture to help combat climate change—the biggest crisis of our time," she says.

Today, Anna Jane is on the other side of that dark moment in her life. She's feeling centered and positive. And she's working hard to tell stories about the climate, infusing what it means to be alive in this moment and time. "That's the driving force at the moment and I think it will certainly be for the rest of my life."

Find Anna Jane online:

Twitter: @annajanejoyner

Instagram: @annajanejoyner

Website: https://www.goodenergystories.com/

Jennifer Uchendu: Sustainability Vibes

Jennifer Uchendu's bags are packed. She's headed from her home in Lagos, Nigeria, to Glasgow, Scotland, to attend the most important global climate summit in the world. It's called COP26, also known as the 26th annual meeting of the Conference of Parties to the United Nations Framework Convention on Climate Change.

"We really want to see rapid and urgent action to stop illegal logging," Jennifer says about Nigeria, the most populated country in Africa. This is one of Jennifer's goals at the global United Nations climate summit in 2021.

Some people refer to Nigeria as the Giant of Africa because it's such a vast country with so much diversity and natural resources. More than 250 languages are spoken in Nigeria! You can find deserts, plains, mountains, and jungles there. The

Niger delta, a land mass formed from the deposits of one of the largest river systems in the world, is home to a whopping 31 million people.

Unfortunately, Nigeria has one of the highest deforestation rates in the world. Various companies log forests there to sell timber or raise cattle. And for some communities, wood is their only source of energy for cooking.

Nigeria is one of the largest exporters of rosewood in the world. A cubic meter of kosso—a species of rosewood native to Western Africa—can sell for $50,000 in China. Sadly, illegal loggers have bribed local officials to turn a blind eye to their predatory logging in fragile forests.

Jennifer, an ecofeminist and sustainability communicator from Lagos, is calling for more leaders to act in order to sustain the natural resources in her country. Because of corrupt government decisions and a lack of coherent forest policy—along with few alternative energy sources for communities to thrive—the situation is dire.

"It's such good news to hear leaders committing to stop deforestation by 2030, but we're also used to lots of talk and not much action," Jennifer says. "So really, I won't say that we're successful until we get to 2030 and see how far we've come."

She points out that Africa is responsible for just 3 percent of global emissions yet is one of the most vulnerable regions to climate change in the world. Lagos, Nigeria's largest city, could be uninhabitable by the end of this century if sea levels continue to rise.

Nigeria is also the top oil-producing country in Africa. Yet the profits from the oil industry have trickled down to such a small percentage of the population here. Most people in the main oil region, the Niger Delta, are living in extreme poverty and pollution.

In college, Jennifer got her bachelor's degree in biochemistry and went on to earn certificates in carbon management from the European Energy Centre and Global Reporting Initiative. Today she has a master's in development studies, with a specialization in gender and climate change.

She had not heard of the term *climate anxiety* until she moved to the United Kingdom, where she completed a master's in development studies at the Institute of Development Studies, University of Sussex. Jennifer says that having a phrase to describe her feelings about the changing climate "somehow made them real."

She wanted to understand how climate change and mental health intersect in young people. So she started to write about her fears in a blog called *SustyVibes*, short for "sustainability vibes."

"Climate anxiety is something a lot of young people like me are experiencing," she says. "It's that emotional response to the idea that world leaders, particularly the world leaders in the West—the rich and powerful nations—aren't taking this issue as seriously as they should."

"Young people are frightened, scared, overwhelmed, and angry," Jennifer says. For her, climate anxiety is rooted in anger. She and her fellow activists are rising up to live more sustainably, even though Nigeria contributes a small fraction of a percent of global carbon emissions. She is doing this via a project called TEAP (The Eco-Anxiety Africa Project).

"Why do we have to be the ones vulnerable and so marginalized?" Uchendu says. "When you look at the history of climate change, you just get really angry, because there are layers of oppression, there's racism."

After launching *SustyVibes* Jennifer posted an event to bring people together to talk about sustainability. Her vision was to create a platform for young people in Nigeria to do sustainability work, so she was pleasantly surprised when 50 people showed up to her first meeting in 2016.

"*Sustyvibes* has since become this huge community that's grown beyond me," she says about her platform, which has grown into a youth-led organization that champions sustainable development in Nigeria.

"I believed that humanity stood a chance against climate change," Jennifer says about founding her platform to inspire action from young people in Nigeria. "Considering how much worse things appear to have gotten since 2015, my optimism is being slowly replaced with gloomy reflections of a worn-down planet with crippling life support systems that can trigger resource wars, exacerbate disasters and displace millions of vulnerable people. Studying development has also revealed to me the linkages between social and environmental injustice, where poor, struggling countries in Africa suffer from the impacts of emissions they contributed the least to."

She continues to rise up and advocate for change and action every day. One of the many projects Jennifer leads is assisting youth to plant trees in Nigeria. Thanks to financial support from the British High Commission in Nigeria, she and *Sustyvibes* volunteers planted about 5,000 trees in and around Lagos, Nigeria.

Planting trees is one way to mitigate climate change in Nigeria, Jennifer argues, because "our forests, freshwater, coastal zones, and biodiversity are all at risk of the impacts of the climate crisis," and "Nigerians depend on these for their livelihood."

Jennifer wants international high-level meetings and negotiations, like the ones led by the United Nations, to include youth and their ideas as part of the problem-solving process. This is something that climate activists around the world—especially girls and young women—have been appealing to leaders for for years. Climate change hits women and girls first and worst, particularly in poor communities and the Global South, so these voices need to be part of the solution.

"It has to be all hands on deck to solve the climate crisis, to save the world and save ourselves, too," Jennifer says.

In Africa the stakes are high. The combination of extremely high deforestation rates, increased temperatures, and decreasing rainfall are all contributing to desertification, and local populations often don't have the financial resources to recover from weather emergencies. Wealthier countries need to step up and help finance the fallout from climate change. "As much as we try to make change, I also see government inaction—trees being cut up on the daily," Jennifer says. "Young people are having to suffer the brunt of these issues when crisis or disasters come in."

Jennifer is determined to include youth in decision-making. "The more that young people are aware of the environmental problems, the more concerned they'll be," she says, adding that "it's really important for young people to be included in the planning."

She predicts that change will also happen when more women are empowered. "In Africa and many rural populations, women play critical roles in natural resource management including water, forests, and energy. They often have experience dealing with nature that can be applied to climate change risk prevention."

Women in Nigeria, for example, are pushing for more innovative technologies such as clean cookstoves to help reduce deforestation and illegal tree logging in many parts of the country.

In 2020 during the height of the pandemic, Jennifer got married to a Nigerian street documentary photographer named Bernard Kalu. Together, they are adapting, learning, and digging deeper. COVID-19 added another layer of struggle for everyone.

"What the pandemic taught us was we can take it slow and steady and be really intentional," Jennifer says. "We now have a renewed sense of what climate resilience really is. We're going to press on."

Follow Jennifer Uchendu Online

Website: https://www.sustyvibes.com/

Twitter: @Dzennypha and @SustyVibes

Instagram: @SustyVibes

Trailblazer: Ugochi Anyaka-Oluigbo

In Nigeria journalist Ugochi Anyaka-Oluigbo is a household name for her reporting on environmental issues. On her TV show, *Green Angle*, she's known for being out on the streets with real people.

"I don't just tell stories, I am there with them," Ugochi says. "I'm in the water, I'm in the floods with them, I'm in their homes, I'm sitting down, I'm feeling what they're feeling. I'm experiencing life with them. So that is what they see."

In a podcast episode called "We Don't Have the Power to Fight It," journalist Amy Westervelt (profiled in chapter 2) talks with Ugochi about how "companies like Royal Dutch Shell and other oil companies have left the delta to be what is one of the most polluted places on the planet."

"It's so brutal what's happened there," Amy says. "For decades, Royal Dutch Shell and its Nigerian subsidiary spilled vast amounts of oil into the river and onto the land. They really ruined a way of life for thousands of people in communities that lived by fishing in the Niger."

"The damage has been very well documented for more than a decade, but the oil companies have barely started to clean up the mess they made," Ugochi says, explaining that in 2015, 40,000 people in Niger delta communities brought a lawsuit against Royal Dutch Shell, which the Hague Court of Appeals decided in the residents' favor in January 2021, with Shell ordered to pay an unspecified amount in damages. But for Ugochi a payout isn't enough: "It won't heal the damage the oil companies did on the land and the water. I've been to these places, I've seen them myself, and it's horrible."

Ugochi grew up in Aba, a small commercial city in southern Nigeria that's along the bank of the Aba River. She says that listening to stories from her father as a little girl is what inspired her to become a journalist.

For example, he would explain to her how erosion was affecting their farm and village, and why it was happening. "He planted that seed early," she says. "Then I started hearing about global warming, climate change, and the environment."

Ugochi, who's also the mother of three young children, has won many journalism awards for her work, and she's currently a fellow of the Climate Change Media Partnership.

Ugochi is especially drawn to covering the stories of women in Nigeria. "For African women their lives are altered forever," she says about the climate crisis displacing families. "We have stories of women who have to move with their kids. Sometimes they are doing it all by themselves. We talk to them at the displaced people's camps, and they tell us about having to fend for their family to get firewood or water."

"It's a huge problem for a lot of African women who have to endure the challenges that have been exacerbated by climate change," Ugochi adds.

One of her goals is to train other journalists to report on environmental issues in Africa.

That's why Ugochi cofounded a program in 2018 to convey eco-journalism skills to more reporters. "I want to see more people reporting on the environment," she says. "My dream is to inspire more young people."

Ugochi is determined for the world to hear more stories from Africa: "A lot of Africans say our voices are drowned." But as we hear more stories from people around the world, hopefully we will start asking questions and raise our voices. "We need to demand accountability from the government," Ugochi says.

14

Tessa Khan:
Keep It in the Ground

Environmental injustice describes how people of color and poor communities experience higher rates of pollution and exacerbating systemic inequalities.

An international climate change and human rights lawyer, campaigner, and strategist based in London, Tessa Khan envisions a world in which communities are powered by renewable energy from the sun, Earth's core, wind, and water. "These options definitely exist," says Tessa. "And there's a lot of interest, even among some of the workers in the offshore oil and gas industry in the UK who are shifting to the offshore wind industry, which is a burgeoning industry here."

As governments vow to phase out fossil fuels, they also need to ensure people that they'll have jobs to support themselves and their families. Authentic climate justice isn't merely a pet project for the wealthy. It's about securing a better future for all of us.

This is why Tessa founded the UK-based organization Uplift, where she directs a team to "resource, connect, and elevate ideas and voices to set in motion a just transition away from fossil fuel production."

The United Kingdom is the second-largest oil and gas producer in Europe, Tessa points out. "Planned global oil and gas production will take us far past the climate limits that are safe for our society. At the same time, clean, affordable, and abundant alternatives to fossil fuels continue to race ahead."

Her mission is for a just and fossil fuel–free world, with equity and justice at the heart of everything she does.

In the late '70s Tessa's parents immigrated from Bangladesh to the United Kingdom, where she and her sister were born. From there, they moved to Singapore and then Australia, where Tessa studied from elementary school and through college. "I grew up in Perth, which is the most isolated capital city in the world. It's quite a contrast to Bangladesh." Tessa was a perceptive kid who noticed how different each city was.

During visits back to Bangladesh to see her extended family, Tessa became alert to global inequality. "I couldn't see any good reason why my family in Bangladesh didn't get to experience the quality of life that we did in Australia," she says. "They worked just as hard, and it became clear to me that there was something pretty profoundly wrong with the way that the world works, even if I couldn't really define it or explain it."

In high school Tessa was on the debate team, and she went on to compete nationally. "We won a world debate championship when I was 16," she says, adding that's when she realized that she had a knack and passion for bringing people around to her deeply held convictions.

After getting a degree in political science and law, Tessa left Australia to get her master's in law from the University of Oxford. "When I started to study law, I didn't think that it would be the thing that I ended up using to be an instrument for change," Tessa says. "If we're honest, most lawyers go on to work for big corporate law firms and make a lot of money and basically prop the world up as it is."

Fortunately, along the way, Tessa met some lawyers who worked in human rights and public interest: "They showed me there was a way to use the law as a means to make positive social change."

Tessa decided to become a human rights lawyer so she could advocate for economic equality and justice. In her career, Tessa has worked hard to use the law as a tool to reduce emissions from greenhouse gases. Fossil fuels—coal, oil, and gas—are at the heart of the crises so many people face around the world, including public health, racial injustice, and climate change. This is especially true for Black, Brown, Indigenous, and poor communities, who are disproportionately in danger. Greenpeace calls this "fossil fuel racism."

Tessa is on a mission to protect communities by phasing out oil, gas, and coal. "The global toll of premature deaths attributed to the burning of coal, gasoline, and diesel is breathtakingly high, with new research doubling previous estimates," according to the Natural Resources Defense Council, which was founded in 1970 by a group of law students and attorneys at the forefront of the environmental movement.

Tessa's driving motivation is to support real people on the ground who are most affected by climate change and empower them.

Tessa emphasizes that both governments and industries are responsible for keeping people healthy and safe.

Governments have a legal obligation to take care of humans. That means they are responsible for reducing greenhouse gas emissions that imperil life on our planet. Doing otherwise, in Tessa's words, "is a real betrayal." They have the power to phase out fossil fuels. Yet the gas and oil industry have spent so much time, energy, and countless billions of dollars to downplay the effects and risks of climate change. (For a more detailed picture of how corporate greed has obstructed climate justice, see chapter 2, on Amy Westervelt.)

"Some of them now have these new 'net-zero strategies' that purport to show that they're taking climate change seriously, but if you look more closely at those plans, they often involve increasing fossil fuel production over the next decade," Tessa says.

Net zero? Some corporations and leaders are greenwashing us by suggesting they can use new technologies or plant trees to offset carbon emissions—a "net-zero" strategy—instead of facing the wooly mammoth in the room. The damage has already been done. As long as our economies continue to rely on fossil fuels, we're always going to be teetering on the knife's edge of extinction.

"We need to let our governments know that they've let us down, and that they can't get away with this," Tessa says. "The climate crisis has become a reality all over the world with rising sea levels, heat waves, and wildfires. Burning fossil fuels puts carbon into the atmosphere, and scientists have been telling us for decades that buildup of greenhouse gases causes global warming."

Tessa points out that fossil fuel companies have known since the 1970s that their industries lead directly to global warming. "A government like the UK should be one of the first ones to move away from fossil fuel production and embrace the alternatives," because of both its history and its wealth.

"So that's really what we're trying to encourage the government to do," Tessa says. "But fighting for the future is about more than keeping governments accountable. "The other big group that's responsible is the fossil fuel industry. We should do everything in our power to hold them accountable, too."

In 2015 Tessa was living in Thailand and working for a non-profit that supported women's rights when she heard about a case on the other side of the world in which hundreds of Dutch citizens had brought a lawsuit against their government in the Netherlands, demanding that their leaders reduce greenhouse gas emissions. They were part of a group called Urgenda, and Tessa was excited to join them. (The name *Urgenda* is a blend of the words *urgent* and *agenda*.)

The case went to the High Council of the Netherlands and would be the first case in the world to force a national government to address climate change in order to uphold its human rights commitments.

In a separate case, lawyers brought evidence that Royal Dutch Shell—the parent company of the global Shell group—is intensifying the climate crisis.

Shell argued "that it is simply responding to continued demand for oil and gas," but Tessa pointed out that this is essentially like drug dealers blaming their customers for the drug epidemic.

In the end, Shell lost! This was a huge turning point in the fight against big oil. Tessa explains, "The court held that Shell's current policy of merely reducing the 'carbon intensity' of its products by 20% by 2030, and aiming to reach net zero by 2050, would contribute to climate impacts that endanger the human rights of the plaintiffs."

"The oil giants that have helped drive the climate crisis are finally being forced to take responsibility for their actions," Tessa triumphantly proclaims.

But the fight is not over. There's an oil field called Cambo that's off the Shetland Islands in the North Atlantic. This region is owned by Shell and another company called Ithaca Energy. They've been planning for years to exploit this field for oil exploration.

In the first phase alone, these companies want to extract up to 170 million barrels of oil, which would generate emissions equivalent to the annual carbon pollution from 18 coal-fired power stations. In order to go ahead with these oil and gas projects, these companies need government approval.

Tessa's organization coordinated the #StopCambo campaign. "The UK government is about to open a massive new oil field," declared UK climate activists from #StopCambo. "We're here to stop them. . . . If we want a livable climate, we can't allow any new oil and gas extraction."

"The UN and International Energy Agency agree we can't have new oil and gas developments in a world in which we limit warming to 1.5°C. It's as simple as that," Tessa says.

Thanks to Tessa and the UK climate activists who rose up, this huge oil project was paused. This was one of the biggest climate wins in 2021.

"There is now broad understanding that there can be no new oil and gas projects anywhere if we're going to maintain a safe climate," Tessa says.

However, the struggle continues. "Governments are already on track to produce double the volume of fossil fuels that we can burn if we are going to preserve a livable climate."

"The battle is not over yet," Tessa adds. She shines a spotlight on the oil and gas projects the UK government is still considering, calling them "indefensible."

"We need Cambo stopped for good and a real plan to support a just transition for oil and gas workers and their communities," the #StopCambo campaign says on Instagram. "Only the government can do this. We can't leave it up to the market or the whims of oil and gas company execs."

"Instead of opening new oil and gas fields that tether us to fossil fuel infrastructure and lock in decades of emissions," Tessa adds, "we should redirect our resources and energy towards an ambitious transition plan with affected workers and communities at its heart."

At the end of the day, it's people who are suffering from the effects of climate change, Tessa points out. Workers in the oil and gas industry are worried about how they'll support their families if they transition into a new industry. But in an extensive survey of 1,500 people who work in the oil and gas industry in the United Kingdom, performed by one of Uplift's partners, they also related worries about their health and the future for their children.

"Governments and oil and gas companies will—and are being—held accountable by people all over the world who know exactly who is to blame for the climate crisis and the unavoidable implication of all those promises to preserve our climate: we have to keep fossil fuels in the ground," Tessa says.

Tessa is incredibly motivated to change and committed to making the world a place where people can live and thrive. "I really care deeply about people in the world that we live in, and about our future," she says.

Follow Tessa Khan Online

Website: https://upliftuk.org/ and https://stopcambo .org.uk

Twitter: @tessakhan

Trailblazer: Newsha Ajami

"Water is an essential resource that we cannot live without," says Newsha Ajami, a leading expert in sustainable water resource management in the San Francisco Bay Area.

Today, as the director of urban water policy with Stanford University's Water in the West, Newsha asks questions like, Where has all of the water gone?

"Everybody is so excited about reducing carbon emissions," she says. "But sometimes we forget about water. If we don't seriously incorporate water into the climate discussion and actions, we actually might not really have much of a future."

Newsha, who was born and raised in Tehran, Iran, studied civil engineering in college. "There were three girls in my civil engineering class, and 80 boys!" By the time Newsha enrolled in a master's program, she was the only woman.

She got an invitation to study hydrology and water resources at the University of Arizona, and then received her PhD in civil and environmental engineering from University of California, Irvine.

Today, she's considered an expert on water policy and rethinking how we can do things differently to manage water demand. She also serves on the San Francisco Public Utilities Commission to help the city rethink its water, wastewater, and energy strategies.

"Water consumption should be at the heart of every discussion we're having because water is a limited resource," Newsha says. "The less we use, the less we pollute, and the more we can leave for our ecosystem to survive."

In most parts of the Global North, for example, we use clean water to flush our toilets. If we simply reused water—say, from our showers—to flush our toilets, we'd be reusing one-quarter of the water in our homes!

"We've set up our water system in a way that leads to heedless water usage," Newsha says. "We discard water after using it once."

Infrastructure does not have to be an obstacle or a barrier, in Newsha's estimation. "What we built in the past century was based on the knowledge and capacity we had then," she says, referring to, for example, how the Western world designed and built structures with water pipes and pumps that simply flushed water away. "We did this to the best of our knowledge. And now we have seen the consequences of some of those decisions."

"At the end of the day, water is at the heart of the resources we need to survive. We should be very mindful of how we're preserving and using it."

In 2021 California experienced the second-driest year on record in history. "There used to be at least 10 years in between major record-breaking droughts in California, which was enough time for our ecosystems to recover," Newsha says.

That's no longer true. So in 2021, California governor Gavin Newsom declared a drought emergency for most counties in California and set up statewide rules to ban the wasting of water. For example, you can be fined $500 for watering lawns within 48 hours after a rainstorm. Or for hosing off your driveway.

"These are no-brainers," according to Newsha. "I'm glad they are being implemented. I wish they would have done it months ago." Newsha works hard to make cities "smarter" by using data science principles to study the human and policy dimensions of urban water and hydrologic systems.

There's still time to fix the inefficiencies in our current system: "We definitely can do a lot more just to make sure we use every drop of water properly. And if we do all the right things, we can survive. But if we don't, we can actually have a serious breakdown in the system."

We're capable of change. Newsha is confident that if we invest in climate-safe and resilient infrastructure, we can achieve a sustainable and resilient water future.

In 2022 Newsha accepted a new job to join Lawrence Berkeley National Laboratory as its chief research strategy and development officer for the Earth and Environmental Sciences Area. She continues to be a leading expert in sustainable water resource management.

Anushka Saia Bhaskar:
No Justice, No Peace

Anushka Saia Bhaskar headed to the beach for a fifth-grade field trip in Southern California. When her class walked out to the shore, their teacher gave them a set of tools for an activity in the sand. Anushka sat down with a group of classmates as shovels and buckets were passed around.

"We took a little rope that was one square meter and lined it up on the sand," Anushka says. "Then, we took a shovel and scooped up the sand from the layer off the top from that one square. We used a bucket and a sieve to shake out the sand to see what plastic we could find."

Ten-year-old Anushka was shocked to see how many tiny little plastic bits were in the sieve. How did all of this plastic get here? And what happens when these little pieces of plastic drift back into the water?

"I thought, I can't believe that we as human beings were doing this. It didn't make sense."

This experience opened Anushka's eyes. She was only in elementary school, but Anushka realized that "human beings were harming the environment that we depend on!"

Anushka was determined to do something. She heard about an organization in Long Beach, California, called Algalita that was helping to clean up the ocean, so her teacher called to see if they needed any volunteers.

A man who calls himself Captain Charles Moore founded Algalita after he'd discovered a massive patch of plastic twice the size of Texas floating in the Pacific Ocean in 1997! Today, we all know how this "plastic soup" got into the ocean: our consumption habits have spiraled out of control.

First, Anushka became a peer adviser for the Plastic Ocean Pollution Solution (POPS) youth summit, and soon after, she became Algalita's youth ambassador.

For almost five years, Anushka was Algalita's spokesperson for youth within the movement. She worked with the team, spoke at panels, and helped organize events.

"Algalita has changed my life in many ways, but most of all it has helped me and other youth like me to find a confident voice," she says. "My work as youth ambassador has made me a more confident, inspired, and passionate individual with an improved leadership toolkit. I have learned to be an informed and involved citizen and I am prepared to fight for a future where problems like plastic pollution are extinct."

Anushka realized early on that her mission is to demand action and be an agent for change with and for other young people. "We joke that I was the guinea pig, as the first young voice in the organization who talked to other youth," she says. "I was fortunate to work with hundreds of students all over the world and was regularly motivated by their dedication and enthusiasm for solving the environmental crisis."

Around this time, Anushka also watched a documentary made by journalist and filmmaker Angela Sun called *Plastic Paradise*. It's about Angela's personal journey investigating the Great Pacific Garbage Patch in one of the most remote places on earth. The film sheds light on the effects of our rabid plastic consumption and features a scene discussing the negative health effects of plastic use and plastic pollution.

"This movie really further opened my eyes," Anushka says. "I was shocked to see that the use of plastic products throughout their life cycle relates to issues of human health. Endocrine disrupting chemicals in these products, for example, leach into our lives and into our ecosystems. There was clearly a systemic nature to this problem."

By middle school, she was speaking up in local city council meetings, pleading with adults to ban Styrofoam and plastic bags. "It is easier to defend our ways rather than change them," she said to an auditorium full of people in Huntington Beach.

Plastic or Planet?

The United States is the world's biggest plastic polluter.

Americans generate on average between four and a half and six pounds of solid waste every day—which is between two and eight times the waste in many countries.

For decades, people have been pointing out that recycling doesn't work. Since 1950 only 9 percent of the world's plastic waste has been recycled. It ends up in the landfills . . . or in the ocean. Some people around the world still burn plastic.

Unfortunately, plastic consumption increased in the United States during the COVID-19 pandemic. To tackle plastic pollution, we need big, systemic change. We need to stop producing and using plastic bags and all single-use plastic products.

Organizations like the Sierra Club are calling for a ban on all sales and distribution of certain single-use plastic products right now and for a moratorium on new plastic-producing facilities.

Youth-led international groups like Bye Bye Plastic Bags—started by two young sisters in Bali—are calling for policies and regulations to stop making single-use plastics. Their advocacy and petition for six years played a part in the Bali government's decision to place a ban on all single-use plastics in 2018.

Growing up, Anushka Bhaskar spent the school year in Orange County, California—just an hour south of Los Angeles—and summers in Delhi, India, where her grandparents live. It was such a contrast to go from the suburbs, where she was an avid Girl Scout, to the massive, sprawling city in northern India.

"There's so much pollution in Delhi. Air pollution, water pollution, and waste management problems," Anushka says. "I saw it all firsthand."

Due to the smog, they had to keep all the windows closed to help protect the health of her paternal grandfather, her *dadapapa*, who suffered from asthma. Her maternal grandfather, her *nana*, was a civil engineer who'd helped clean up the Ganges and evacuate villagers during a huge flood. Both of her grandfathers have inspired her work and vision for the future. When her nana, "the healthiest 74-year-old we knew," died of colon cancer after a long battle with his disease, Anushka realized just how passionate she was about issues of human health and the environment.

She adds that her years in the Girl Scouts empowered her to start speaking up for her community. Anushka was one of 12 girls in the country to be chosen as a National Girl Innovator, whom the Girl Scouts of the USA train to facilitate groups, strategize, and organize events.

"Having those experiences led to much of my work today," she says. Through Girl Scouts, she met her mentor, Kelly Vlahakis-Hanks, president and CEO of Earth Friendly Products.

Teens on the Front Lines of Change

Lola Guthrie, a 17-year-old from Sebastopol, California, was one of seven youth activists with the Sunrise Movement who marched during the summer of 2021 for 266 miles (428 km) from Paradise to San Francisco.

Lola, who has lived through multiple wildfires, says that she's "no longer comforted by the thought that adults will clean up their mess. I feel outraged and hopeless."

That's why she and young people all over the country have been pressuring US legislators to support the establishment of a Civilian Climate Corps (CCC). The CCC would employ thousands of young people to address the threat of climate change, strengthen the country's natural defenses, and maintain its ailing public lands. The CCC would also invest back into communities, stimulate the economy, provide work to the unemployed and underemployed, reduce wildlife damages, and more.

"No one can deny that fossil fuel executives have subverted our democracy's ability to protect our students, communities, and young teachers from fossil fuel pollution and climate neglect," says Lola's dad, Park Guthrie, a sixth-grade teacher in California and father of three.

Park says his children, along with young people around the world, have experienced "generational climate abandonment."

In October 2021 one of Lola's high school friends who'd also marched with her in California—18-year-old Ema

Govea—began a hunger strike at the White House to help break the political power of the fossil fuel industry.

Ema and four other activists stopped eating, with the hope their hunger protest would draw attention to climate change action, specifically after President Joe Biden had said he was going to water down his commitments to environmental legislation.

"Ema is understandably daunted at the burden she has shouldered—a burden so many adult institutions have denied, delayed, or ignored," Park says after seeing Ema before she headed to Washington, DC.

Ema emphasized that young people had elected Biden. "We turned out, going door-to-door. We wrote letters, we campaigned for him. . . . Every day, every month, every year we don't take action is devastating," she says. "Millions of peoples' lives are resting on it."

In 2018 Anushka accepted an offer to attend Harvard. As an undergrad, she took her activism with her. One of the first things she did was speak up about plastic pollution. Joined by her sister, Anchal, they emailed all of their senators, imploring them to make policy changes about plastic waste.

"We're very close," Anushka says about her sister, who's two years younger. "We fight a lot, but we also love each other a lot. We've been able to bond and also find our own spaces."

Her sister traveled with her to the Massachusetts State House to testify in support of a bill to establish a Plastic Pollution Action Day. "Most important was the fact that we were able to make such great connections with our state legislators," Anushka says.

One day at school, Anushka approached the Harvard Office for Sustainability and told them that she wanted to organize a student-led environmental action and leadership summit.

"At first, they didn't totally believe me, to be quite frank. They didn't believe that I could pull it off. And so, I was like, 'OK, I hear you.'"

This was not new to Anushka. As a teen, adults had dismissed her before. Or even ignored her. But Anushka refused to let anyone quiet her. "I want young kids to know that you don't have to wait to be a changemaker. I knew that I didn't have to wait to be an adult, or to have a degree to be a changemaker."

She reached out to Kelly Vlahakis-Hanks and asked if Kelly would help her bring together a community of more than just speakers—"people who are willing to interact with the students and help train them."

Then Anushka went back to Harvard and said, "Look, I have an amazing, values-driven company that's ready to back me in my work and they believe in me."

In the end, about 100 people came to the student-led environmental action and leadership summit, including Sal

DiDomenico, the assistant majority leader of the Massachusetts state senate. Organizing this summit showed Anushka what she's capable of: leading and bringing people together to connect and collaborate for the future.

The CEO of Earth Friendly Products said she was "thrilled to be part of this groundbreaking event to highlight the important role that business must play in being a champion for change and finding innovative solutions alongside our youth leaders."

Anushka had plans for another conference at Harvard, but COVID-19 changed those plans. She moved back in with her family in California for the lockdown from 2019 to 2021. From home, she continued to advocate online for the environment, shifting her focus from plastic pollution to the intersection of human and environmental health. "I have so much energy for this work!" she says.

Every week, Anushka and other youth climate activists message each other and stay in touch. Anushka was invited to serve on the Intersectional Environmentalist Council by her friend Leah Thomas, a writer and author who coined the term *intersectional environmentalism*, a form of environmentalism that works for the advancement of justice for people (particularly people of color) and the planet.

Intersectional environmentalism has long been key to Anushka's approach to environmental advocacy. It "reminds us that our efforts to address environmental problems and their deep interconnections with issues of health should also bring us to discussions of equity. We should not shy away from discussing how systems of oppression such as racism play a role in exacerbating environmental and health inequity."

Her real life and studies collided as she realized that the climate crisis is really a health crisis. "I've always known that I wanted to focus on the environment and health, but I never saw a space where I could connect them," she says. "Especially with my interest in creating better systems of healthcare, it seemed too complicated to intertwine them. I soon realized that there is no way forward without acknowledging the importance of climate justice in creating systems of health justice."

Anushka is currently double-majoring in government and biology in her junior year at Harvard, with a certificate in data science and a minor in global health and health policy. She's on the road to becoming a doctor, with plans to go into medicine and health policy so she can work on addressing the climate crisis as a health crisis and help to improve systems of healthcare in light of the environmental crises we face. "The separation of health and environmental policy is a dangerous mistake, as human health depends entirely on the climate and the natural world."

From her bedroom in Orange County, Anushka founded her own organization called Avritah, an intersectional platform for action dedicated to addressing environmental and health inequity. The word *avritah* loosely translates to "environment" in Sanskrit, an ancient Indian language. Literally, *avritah* means "that which encircles us, or that which is all around us."

Anushka's initial motivation for Avritah was to help people connect health justice with environmental justice. "More and more people are going to be suffering in their health because of climate change." That's why she is working "to build a curriculum for premed and health-interested folks, creating conversation in healthcare communities around health injustice, environmental injustice, and appropriate courses of action."

Anushka looks up to women like Mona Hana-Attisha, one of the doctors responsible for uncovering the Flint water crisis. She feels that practicing medicine in the future will only become further entwined with issues of health justice and environmental justice. She hopes to help train herself and future generations of practitioners to recognize the signs of disease while also looking to help restore environments supporting wellness.

"I don't think many students of health and medicine are getting exposure to how we can concretely play a role in addressing the climate crisis, which is one of the biggest public health threats that we as humanity will ever face. This is a blind spot, and it will require a community of passionate people to figure it out."

Back in person at Harvard, Anushka says she's stronger, happier, and more resilient as she aims to advance her learning and contributions through school and Avritah. While the pandemic undoubtedly presented her with challenges, she knows that there were equally many opportunities for growth. "Just another reminder from the universe that discomfort often supports growth," she says. In her work, studies, and beyond, Anushka hopes to always serve her local and global community with love.

Follow Anushka Saia Bhaskar Online

Website: https://www.avritah.org

Instagram: @anushkasaia

Trailblazer: Violet Wulf-Saena

"We really need to change the system," says Violet Wulf-Saena, founder and executive director of Climate Resilient Communities in Palo Alto, CA.

Violet was born and raised in Samoa, where she was the country's original climate change officer. She created the country's first resiliency plan, when she worked with the Lano and Saoluafata Indigenous peoples to restore coastline ecosystems to try to slow incoming waves and protect communities from storm and flood damage.

After moving to the San Francisco Bay Area, Violet saw that the communities of color in California also experienced the same threats from rising sea levels.

"I see a lot of disparities," Violet says, explaining that there are so many inequalities in the Bay Area. For example, the neighborhoods in East Palo Alto are diverse, low-income, and underresourced communities, in contrast to the nearby prosperous, booming neighborhoods next door that house wealthy companies like Google and Apple.

Violet founded Climate Resilient Communities in 2020 to meet the needs of residents in diverse, underresourced communities in East Palo Alto and Belle Haven, Menlo Park. One of Violet's goals is to try to restore marshlands and wetlands to protect vulnerable neighborhoods.

In 2022, Climate Resilient Communities recruited Youth Climate Fellows between the ages of 12 and 18 in the Bay Area for a six-month paid internship to support communities hands-on. "What really makes a difference is seeing the commitment to policies with funding," she says, explaining that many communities still struggle with basic needs to live, such as clean air, safe drinking water, sufficient food, and secure shelter.

Violet is hopeful that she can help communities prepare for and recover from climate emergencies. "These communities are resilient," she says. "They're still here, and they're still fighting. They have so much to offer."

Acknowledgments

I acknowledge that this book was written on land stolen from Native Americans, specifically from the Confederated Villages of Lisjan, who are part of the Ohlone tribes.

Thank you to every climate champion I interviewed for this book. You taught me so much, lifted me up, encouraged me to ask questions, and kept me going during anxious times. I'm so grateful to you for trusting me.

Thank you to Kara Rota, executive editor at Chicago Review Press, for being such a light in my life! You've been here for me through the pandemic, parenting, and panicked days.

Deep gratitude to cover designer and illustrator Sadie Teper and copyeditor Alexander Caputo.

A great appreciation to the amazing people at Chicago Review Press for all of your thoughtful edits, design, illustrations, marketing, publicity, and more: Benjamin Krapohl, Alayna Parsons-Valles, Devon Freeny, Stefani Szenda, and Valerie Pedroche.

An enormous thank you to Eric Myers, my agent, for being on my team and correcting those dangling modifiers.

Thank you to all my kind, open-hearted, thoughtful readers. I see you.

Thank you to the Institute of Journalism and Natural Resources for the grant that allowed me to travel for a couple of interviews during COVID.

Big thanks to these brilliant, supportive writers who sustain me and keep me accountable: Alex Giardino, Mae Respicio, Angela Dalton, Laura Atkins, Susie Meserve, Sharon Eberhardt, Roberta Gibson, Suzanne LaFetra Collier, Alexandra Ballard, Amelinda Bérubé, Tamara Mahmood Hayes, Wendy McKee, Shellie Faught, Catey Miller, Melissa Mazzone, Bree Barton, Jacqueline Lipton, TJ Ohler, Alison Cherry, Veronica Chater, Katherine Briccetti, B. Lynn Goodwin, Annie Kassof, and Sybil Lockhart.

And also . . . shout out to all of the mamas who continue to hold me and check in: Desiree Ong, Arden Fredman, Siobhan van Winkel, Kellie Lund, Ariel Lustig, Dan Lucido, Payal Sampat, Kirsten Mahoney, Diane Friedlaender, Amy Bremenstuhl, Tonya Delaney Cauduro, Leila Cranford, Christin Weber, Amanda Dora Riesman, Elise Brewin, Sheila Brewin, Rachel Anderson, Céline Farchi, Stéphanie Regni, Rachel Goldman-Stewart, and Raissa Lerner.

Much love to these independent bookstores in the Bay Area: Great Good Place for Books, Pegasus, Books, Inc., and Book Passage.

All the hugs and kisses to my daughters, Mae and Camille, such creative, brave, adventurous, nature-loving warriors at my side.

I'm grateful to Chris, my partner, for holding me and listening to me and keeping the coffee warm.

My mom, Maureen Micus Crisick, a poet who has continued to encourage me to write from the day I picked up a pencil.

And finally, to . . . Aunt Marge, whom we lost the same week I turned in this book. An avid gardener and community leader, your memory lives on.

Resources

Many of the stories in this book reference climate organizations, publications, podcasts, and more that might interest you:

Organizations

350.org: An international movement of ordinary people working to end the age of fossil fuels and build a world of community-led renewable energy for all.
350.org

Amazon Watch: Protecting the rainforest and our climate in solidarity with Indigenous peoples.
amazonwatch.org

Black in Marine Science: Celebrating Black marine scientists, spreading environmental awareness, and inspiring the next generation of scientific thought leaders.
blackinmarinescience.org

Children vs Climate Crisis: Sixteen children from across the world are petitioning the United Nations Committee on the Rights of the Child to hold five of the world's leading economic powers accountable for inaction on the climate crisis.
childrenvsclimatecrisis.org

Citizens' Climate Lobby: 500+ local US chapters, and their sole purpose is to lobby Congress for bipartisan climate policies.
citizensclimatelobby.org

Climate Cardinals: International youth-led nonprofit with 8,000 volunteers in 41 countries working to translate climate information into 105+ languages.
climatecardinals.org

Climate Justice Alliance: Uniting frontline communities and organizations on real-world projects that center traditional ecological and cultural knowledge.
climatejusticealliance.org

Earth Uprising: "Earth Uprising isn't an organization. It's a battle cry. We are young people across the world who won't stay silent while our future is destroyed."
earthuprising.org

Fair Fight Action: Fighting for free and fair elections for all—in Georgia and nationwide.
fairfight.com

Fridays for Future: A youth-led and organized movement that began in August 2018, after 15-year-old Greta Thunberg and other young activists sat in front of the Swedish parliament every school day for three weeks to protest against lack of action on the climate crisis.
fridaysforfuture.org

Fund Her: Political action committee powering progressive women to lead our states, with an emphasis on supporting women of color and LGBTQ candidates.
fundher.org

The Grey Water Project: Promotes the safe reuse of grey water and water conservation in order to create a more sustainable water future for everyone. The nonprofit was founded in 2016 by climate activist and Stanford student Shreya Ramachandran.
thegreywaterproject.org

Heirs to Our Oceans: Youth leaders dedicated to inspire awareness, responsibility, and action among youth worldwide to protect the waters of our Blue Planet.
h2oo.org

Minorities in Shark Sciences (MISS): Founded by four Black female shark researchers to be seen and take up space "in a discipline which has been largely inaccessible for women like us. We strive to be positive role models for the next generation. We seek to promote diversity and inclusion in shark science and encourage women of color to push through barriers and contribute knowledge in marine science."
www.misselasmo.org

Ocean Heroes Bootcamp: For youth between the ages of 9 and 20. Cofounded by Lonely Whale and Captain Planet Foundation.
www.lonelywhale.org

Outdoor Alliance: works to protect the places we ski, hike, climb, paddle, and bike.
www.outdooralliance.org

Polluters Out: Founded after COP25, "a symptom of a much greater and prolonged issue in which the fossil fuel industry controls every aspect of our society from indigenous lands, governments, banks, universities, and climate negotiations."
pollutersout.org

Reserva: The Youth Land Trust: Empowering young people to make a measurable difference for threatened species

and habitats through conservation, education, and story-telling.
reservaylt.org

Science Moms: If you are a mom who cares about climate change, this is a non-partisan group of climate scientists and mothers.
sciencemoms.com

Sunrise Movement: A movement to stop climate change and create millions of good-paying jobs in the process.
sunrisemovement.org

This Is Zero Hour: Youth-led movement that centers the voices of diverse youth in the conversation around climate and environmental justice.
thisiszerohour.org

V-DAY: To end violence against all women, girls, and the planet.
www.vday.org

Vote Save America: One-stop-shop for everything you need to vote, volunteer, and fight for the issues that matter most.
votesaveamerica.com

Youth Advocates for Climate Action Philippines: Leading the ongoing global struggle against climate change on the basis of five points of unity: climate justice, urgency of climate action, defending environmental defenders, youth-led collective action, systemic change.
yacap.org

YouthTopia: Bringing young people together, igniting their passions, and growing their skills to become active change-makers with peer-to-peer programs off- and online.
youthtopia.world

Podcasts

Hot Take: A look "at the climate crisis and all the ways we're talking—and not talking—about it. We take a feminist, race-forward lens to the biggest story of our time. Some people might call it intersectional, we call it honest. Cohosted by Mary Annaïse Heglar and Amy Westervelt."

Drilled: "A true-crime podcast about climate change, hosted and reported by award-winning investigative journalist Amy Westervelt."

How to Save a Planet: "Climate change. We know. It can feel too overwhelming. But what if there was a show about climate change that left you feeling . . . energized? One so filled with possibility that you actually wanted to listen? Join us, journalist

Alex Blumberg and a crew of climate nerds, as we bring you smart, inspiring stories about the mess we're in and how we can get ourselves out of it."

Broken Ground: "A podcast by the Southern Environmental Law Center. Join us as we dig up environmental stories in the South and hear from the people bringing those stories to light."

The Climate Question: Produced by BBC World Service, each episode is a question the team tries to answer about climate change: "how best to understand it and the world's attempts to avert it, temper it or adapt to it. It is not about questioning whether climate change is happening, it's about finding the best ways to respond to it."

Recommended Reading

Amy Westervelt: *Forget "Having It All": How America Messed Up Motherhood—and How to Fix It*

Beth Shapiro: *Life as We Made It: How 50,000 Years of Human Innovation Refined—and Redefined—Nature*

Katharine Hayhoe: *Saving Us: A Climate Scientist's Case for Hope and Healing in a Divided World*

Amy Cardinal Christianson: *First Nations Wildfire Evacuations: A Guide for Communities and External Agencies* and *Blazing the Trail: Celebrating Indigenous Fire Stewardship.*

Jeanette Davis: *Jada's Journey Under the Sea* and *Science Is Everywhere: Science Is for Everyone* (picture books)

Ayana Elizabeth Johnson and Katharine K. Wilkinson, editors: *All We Can Save: Truth, Courage, and Solutions for the Climate Crisis*

Notes

Introduction

"Earth is running a fever": CCNOW, "Climate Science 101," Climate Science Now, March 28, 2021, https://coveringclimatenow.org/resource /climate-science-101/.

Chapter 1: Molly Kawahata

ice in the darkness: Molly Kawahata, "What a Weekend!" Instagram, June 22, 2021, https://www.instagram.com/p/CQZVM2uDYAf/.

"I'm not a morning person": All quotes from original author interview with Molly Kawahata on February 26, 2021, unless otherwise noted here.

Obama at a rally: CNN Newsroom, "President-elect Takes Historic Train Ride in Washington" (transcript), CNN, aired January 7, 2009, http:// www.cnn.com/TRANSCRIPTS/0901/17/cnr.01.html; Cathy Cockrell, "Obama Youth Leader Takes a Detour," UC Berkeley News, August 25, 2008, https://www.berkeley.edu/news/media/releases/2008/08/25 _kawahata.shtml; Ingrid Hu Dahl, "What Youth Journalists Heard from Their Peers About This Election," Youth Media Reporter, October 27, 2008, https://www.youthmediareporter.org/2008/10/27 /what-youth-journalists-heard-from-their-peers-about-this-election/.

"average person struggling": Molly Kawahata, "Climate Change Is Not About Saving the Planet," Instagram, April 23, 2021, https://www.instagram .com/p/CN_p4TpjMfo/.

"change the system": Greta Thunberg, "COP24 Speech," YouTube video, posted by Fridays for Future, December 12, 2018, https://youtu.be /watch?v=CcQp_l7WqAk.

What is systemic change?: "Systematic vs. Systemic: There's a System to the Difference," Dictionary.com June 16, 2020, https://www.dictionary.com/e/systematic-vs-systemic/?itm_source=parsely-api.

"I sort of misunderstood the question": Molly Kawahata, "Today Is the Groundbreaking," Instagram, September 29, 2021, https://www.instagram.com/p/CUYL374PFyf/.

"I got to meet Molly on a trip to Washington, DC": All quotes within "Trailblazer: Caroline Gleich" sidebar from original author interview with Caroline Gleich on November 1, 2021, unless otherwise noted here.

"lost my half-brother": Caroline Gleich, "When I Was 15," Instagram, November 19, 2021, accessed on August 24, 2022, https://www.instagram.com/p/CWcLrpxra24/. For more about Caroline's story, see "Professional Skier: Caroline Gleich," Clif Bar, accessed on August 24, 2022, https://www.clifbar.com/athletes/caroline-gleich.

"Public lands can and should": Caroline Gleich, "Making Public Lands Part of Climate Solutions," Outdoor Alliance, February 26, 2020, https://www.outdooralliance.org/blog/2020/2/26/making-public-lands-part-of-climate-solutions.

"an outlier in the climbing world": Chris Gayomali, "Why Working Out with Other People Is So Powerful," *GQ*, June 2, 2021, https://www.gq.com/story/nyc-athletic-crews.

"When people find out that I climb": Ashima Shiraishi, "Just Climb Through It," YouTube video, posted by TEDx Talks, October 22, 2014, https://www.youtube.com/watch?v=dIz7n7KWlZY.

"possibly the best": Nick Paumgarten, "The Wall Dancer," *New Yorker*, January 3, 2016, https://www.newyorker.com/magazine/2016/01/11/the-wall-dancer.

She's also vegan: "Who Is Ashima Shiraishi?—Making History from Age 8," Climber News, July 6, 2021, https://www.climbernews.com/who-is-ashima-shiraishi/.

Chapter 2: Amy Westervelt

"I can count on one hand": All quotes from original author interview with Amy Westervelt on June 15, 2021, unless otherwise noted here.

juggling work deadlines: Amy Westervelt, "The Uses of Sorrow, November 15, 2021, *No Place like Home* (podcast), season 4, episode 1, https://open.spotify.com/show/6DuuXYg5XcluBtcOE1Klis; and

Amy Westervelt, Twitter post, August 23, 2021, https://twitter.com/amywestervelt/status/1429586730915487746.

massive August Complex: Priya Krishnakumar and Swetha Kannan, "The Worst Fire Season Ever. Again," *Los Angeles Times*, September 15, 2020, https://www.latimes.com/projects/california-fires-damage-climate-change-analysis/.

"still seemed pretty abstract": Amy Westervelt, "We Don't Have the Power to Fight It," transcript, *Scene on Radio* (podcast), season 5, episode 6, http://www.sceneonradio.org/wp-content/uploads/2021/11/S5E6_transcript1_FINAL.pdf.

"He convinced my mom": Amy Westervelt, *Forget "Having It All": How America Messed Up Motherhood—and How to Fix It* (New York: Seal Press, 2018), 246.

"Now his VA benefits": Amy Westervelt, Twitter post, August 2018: https://twitter.com/amywestervelt/status/1030845443746422784.

"over-aged intern": Lauren Passell, "🎙️q & a & q & a & q & a👏": Amy Westervelt," Podcast The Newsletter, January 4, 2021 https://podcastthenewsletter.substack.com/p/-the-day-the-nba-shut-down-disney.

"If you're looking for" through *"We take a feminist, race-forward lens"*: "About Us," Hot Take (website), accessed August 8, 2022, https://www.hottakepod.com/about-us/.

"thinking, Climate denial?": "A Crisis, a Cover-up, and a Community on the Front Lines of Climate Change," transcript, April 2019, *Drilled* (podcast), season 2, episode 1, https://www.desmog.com/s2ep1-crisis-cover-and-community-front-lines-climate-change/; Amy Westervelt, "Podcasts That Make the Climate Crisis Personal: A New Generation of Audio Storytellers Meet Global Warming," *Sierra*, September 27, 2021, https://www.sierraclub.org/sierra/2021-4-fall/critic-s-notebook/podcasts-make-climate-crisis-personal; "Amy Westervelt: The Use of PR Firms in Obstructing Climate Action," talk at Brown University, December 3, 2021, YouTube video, https://www.youtu.be/watch?v=SJutTNqxOs4.

"has transformed climate journalism": Eric Holthaus, Twitter post, October 19, 2020, https://twitter.com/ericholthaus/status/1317894376652230657.

"'came out of nowhere'": Amy Westervelt, Twitter post, November 5, 2019, https://twitter.com/amywestervelt/status/1195392160004104192; Amy Westervelt, "Climate Rage Is Sexy," Hot Take (website), February 14, 2021, https://www.hottakepod.com/climate-rage-is-sexy-651/.

"fed a false narrative": Georgia Wright, Liat Olenick, and Amy Westervelt, "The Dirty Dozen: Meet America's Top Climate Villains," *Guardian*,

October 27, 2021, https://www.theguardian.com/commentisfree
/2021/oct/27/climate-crisis-villains-americas-dirty-dozen.

"don't live near extended family": Amy Westervelt, "Mothering in the Age of
Extinction," Drilled News, June 18, 2020, https://www.drilledpodcast
.com/mothering-in-the-age-of-extinction/; Elise Hu, "American
Motherhood Is 'Messed Up,' Author Says. Here's How She Wants
to Fix It," radio broadcast, WBUR, November 13, 2018, https://
www.wbur.org/hereandnow/2018/11/13/forget-having-it-all-amy
-westervelt.

"white-hot rage": Westervelt, "Mothering."

"distributing propaganda": "The First Day at School," September 24, 2021,
Drilled and Earther Present: The ABCs of Big Oil (podcast), episode 1,
https://www.drilledpodcast.com/s7-the-abcs-of-big-oil/.

Chapter 3: Wanjiku "Wawa" Gatheru

"I've felt, as a Black girl": All quotes from original author interview with
Wanjiku "Wawa" Gatheru on February 10, 2021, unless otherwise
noted here.

wounding history that still plagues: "Meet the First Black Rhodes, Truman,
and Udall Scholar," YouTube video, March 2, 2020, https://youtu
.be/watch?v=xXKOUb3KvaY.

"reckon with that legacy": Wanjiku Gatheru, "Environmental Justice & Racism," September 2, 2020, *Lonely Whale* (podcast), episode 3, https://
www.lonelywhale.org/52hertz/againsthecurrent/epsiode3.

"arguably one of the most beautiful": Westport Library "To Be an Environmentalist, Start with Antiracism" (talk), December 17, 2020, https://
youtu.be /watch?v=1tuyXjV17zE&t=567s.

"literally surrounded me": Westport Library, "Start with Antiracism."

"I'll be a doctor": Wanjiku Gatheru and Peggy Shepard, "A Wave of Change,"
Atmos, November 25, 2020, https://atmos.earth/wanjiku-gatheru
-peggy-shepard-interview/.

"worst chemistry student": Westport Library, "Start with Antiracism."

"environmental justice chapter": Fix, "These Environmental Justice Leaders
Are Creating the Spaces They Wish They'd Had," Grist, June 7, 2021,
https://grist.org/fix/these-ej-leaders-are-creating-spaces-environmental
-activism-education/.

cued up a TEDx talk: Peggy Shepard, "Environmental Justice," TEDx Talks,
YouTube video, posted July 31, 2012, https://youtu.be/watch?v=zJX
_MXaXbJA.

asthma rates: Wanjiku Gatheru, "How This 22-Year-Old Is Creating an Anti-racist Climate Movement," interview by Kerry Justich, Yahoo Life, April 21, 2021, https://www.yahoo.com/lifestyle/black-environmentalist -creating-anti-racist-climate-movement-214113532.html.

"connected the dots": Gatheru and Shepard, "Wave of Change."

"If communities of color": Wanjiku Gatheru, "Want to Be an Environmentalist? Start with Antiracism," *Glamour*, July 30, 2020, https://www .glamour.com/story/want-to-be-an-environmentalist-start-with-anti -racism.

"existential threats like climate change": Mary Annaïse Heglar, "We Don't Have to Halt Climate Action to Fight Racism," HuffPost, June 12, 2020, https://www.huffpost.com/entry/climate-crisis-racism -environmenal-justice_n_5ee072b9c5b6b9cbc7699c3d.

"It's no secret": Wanjiku Gatheru, "It's Time for Environmental Studies to Own Up to Erasing Black People," *Vice*, June 12, 2020, https://www .vice.com/en/article/889qxx/its-time-for-environmental-studies-to -own-up-to-erasing-black-people.

"movement's founding fathers": Gatheru, "It's Time for Environmental Studies to Own Up."

"really paved the way": Gatheru and Shepard, "Wave of Change."

"still something that I work through": Gatheru, "Environmental Justice & Racism."

lack of trees: Tony Barboza and Ruben Vives, "Poor Neighborhoods Bear the Brunt of Extreme Heat, 'Legacies of Racist Decision-Making,'" *Los Angeles Times*, October 28, 2021, www.latimes.com/california /story/2021-10-28/extreme-heat-built-environment-equity.

segregated neighborhoods have fewer trees: Joe Purtell, "Planting Trees to Offset the Legacy of Racist Housing Policies," *Salon*, August 28, 2021, https://www.salon.com/2021/08/28/planting-trees-to-offset-the -legacy-of-racist-housing-policies_partner/.

5 to 20 degrees: Brad Plumer and Nadja Popovich, "Housing Policy Left Neighborhoods Sweltering," *New York Times*, August 24, 2020, https://www.nytimes.com/interactive/2020/08/24/climate/racism -redlining-cities-global-warming.html.

much higher pollution: Alejandra Borunda, "How 'Nature Deprived' Neighborhoods Impact the Health of People of Color," *National Geographic*, July 29, 2020, https://www.nationalgeographic.com/science /article/how-nature-deprived-neighborhoods-impact-health-people -of-color.

making greenways: Groundwork USA, "Groundwork USA Network" (web page), accessed on August 24, 2022, https://groundworkusa.org /groundwork-network/.

carbon back in the ground: Openlands, "What We Do" (web page), accessed on August 24, 2022, https://openlands.org/what-we-do/climate-change/.

Illiana tollway: Stacy Meyers, "Why Openlands Has Joined a Lawsuit Against the City of Joliet," Openlands, November 18, 2020, https://openlands .org/2020/11/18/why-openlands-has-joined-a-lawsuit-against-the -city-of-joliet/.

"we are being sidelined": @instagram, Instagram, November 24, 2021, https:// www.instagram.com/p/CWoS53FpUkj/.

"reframe and reimagine": Gatheru, "Environmental Justice & Racism."

Chapter 4: Trimita Chakma

"Greta Thunberg's work is really important": All quotes from original author interview with Trimita Chakma on May 25, 2021, unless otherwise noted here.

Global South is usually used as metaphor: For more, see Walter D. Mignolo, "The Global South and World Dis/Order," *Journal of Anthropological Research* 67, no. 2 (2011): 165–188. https://doi.org/10.3998 /jar.0521004.0067.202.

"increasing dispossession": Gabriel Tripur et al., "The Experiences and Challenges of Tripura Indigenous Youth in Chittagong Hill Tracts, Bangladesh, During COVID-19," UN Envoy on Youth, https:// www.un.org/youthenvoy/2020/08/the-experiences-and-challenges -of-tripura-indigenous-youth-in-chittagong-hill-tracts-bangladesh -during-covid-19/; and Trimita Chakma, *A Rapid Assessment Report: The Impact of COVID-19 on Indigenous and Tribal Peoples in Bangladesh* (Mohammadpur, Dhaka, Bangladesh: Kapaeeng Foundation, June 2020), accessed August 24, 2022, https://www.iwgia.org/images /news/COVID-19/Bangladesh-Kapaeeng/COVID-19_Report_on _IPs_in_Bangladesh_KF.pdf.

"started The Vagina Monologues*"*: "The Vagina Monologues," V-Day, https://www.vday.org/art-activism/the-vagina-monologues/.

"for the bodies of all": "Women = cisgender, transgender, and those who hold fluid identities that are subject to gender-based violence." See https://www.onebillionrising.org/about/campaign/.

70 percent of the world's poor: Baher Kamal, "Can 70% of the World's Poor Celebrate International Women's Day?" Inter Press Service, March 7,

2022, https://www.ipsnews.net/2022/03/can-70-worlds-poor-celebrate
-international-womens-day/.

"She was with us throughout the year": All quotes within "Trailblazer: Hunter Richards" sidebar from original author interview with Hunter Richards on October 1, 2021, unless otherwise noted here.

"empowering to help make space": "Women Engineers from History," Womengineered, February 26, 2021, https://www.womengineered.org/2021/02/26/women-engineers-from-history/.

Hunter graduated from Harvard: "This Is What an Engineer looks Like," May 25, 2018, https://www.womengineered.org/2018/05/25/this-is-what-an-engineer-looks-like/.

"just to meet boys": @womengineered, "Happy Pride from Your Local Queer Engineer!," Instagram, June 12, 2021, https://www.instagram.com/p/CP_lftgj6L6/.

Chapter 5: Tori Tsui

"Companies like CBS and their shareholders": All quotes from original author interview with Tori Tsui on May 6, 2021, unless otherwise noted here.

"busiest intersectional climate activist": Santiago Rodriguez Tarditi, "Eco-Warrior Profile: The Busiest Intersectional Climate Activist in the World," Oxygen Project, November 7, 2020, https://www.theoxygenproject.com/post/eco-warrior-profile-the-busiest-intersectional-climate-activist-in-the-world/.

"the future for our species": "Facts About Our Ecological Crisis Are Incontrovertible. We Must Take Action," *Guardian*, October 26, 2018, https://www.theguardian.com/environment/2018/oct/26/facts-about-our-ecological-crisis-are-incontrovertible-we-must-take-action.

"My humanity is rooted": Tori Tsui, Instagram, November 17, 2021, https://www.instagram.com/p/CWYkhBUsCA5/.

"the world leaders, fossil fuel companies, multinational companies": All quotes within "Trailblazer: Mitzi Jonelle Tan" sidebar from original author interview with Mitzi Jonelle Tan on December 2, 2021, unless otherwise noted here.

"don't want to be afraid": "Mitzi Jonelle Tan, Convenor / International Spokesperson," Youth Advocates for Climate Action Philippines, https://yacap.org/mitzijonelle/.

"where my hope is": Mitzi Jonelle, Instagram, December 2, 2021, https://www.instagram.com/p/CW-zLl_vEjC/.

"Aren't we the stewards who've kept the system going until now?": All quotes within "Trailblazer: Aryana Henthorne" sidebar from original author interview with Aryana Henthorne on October 13, 2021, unless otherwise noted here.

power of food: "Food Sovereignty," SeedChange, https://weseedchange.org /food-sovereignty/.

"those who produce": Declaration of Nyéléni, 2007 Forum for Food Sovereignty, Sélingué, Mali, https://nyeleni.org/IMG/pdf/DeclNyeleni-en .pdf.

coastal development: See https://www.mendocinolandtrust.org/care/salmon -recovery/.

lack of access to traditional lands: Declaration of Nyéléni.

food apartheid: Jacqui Germain, "Food Insecurity on Native Reservations Is Part of a History of Discrimination," *Teen Vogue*, December 1, 2021, https://www.teenvogue.com/story/food-insecurity-native -reservations-why.

"practiced in Indian Country": "Statement from Heather Dawn Thompson," USDA, May 27, 2021. https://www.usda.gov/media/press -releases/2021/05/27/statement-heather-dawn-thompson-director -usda-office-tribal.

Chapter 6: Katharine Hayhoe

"I'm attacked by trolls every single day": All quotes from original author interview with Katharine Hayhoe on March 9, 2021, unless otherwise noted here.

"carbon dioxide traps heat": Katharine Hayhoe, *Saving Us: A Climate Scientist's Case for Hope and Healing in a Divided World* (New York: Atria/One Signal Publishers, 2021), 46.

"planet should be cooling": Hayhoe, 47.

"most serious humanitarian issues": Katharine Hayhoe, "What I Do," http:// www.katharinehayhoe.com/biography/.

"really important part": Hayhoe, *Saving Us*, ix.

"I'm Canadian": Katharine Hayhoe, "The Most Important Thing You Can Do to Fight Climate Change: Talk About It," TED Talk, November 2018, https://www.ted.com/talks/katharine_hayhoe_the_most_important _thing_you_can_do_to_fight_climate_change_talk_about_it/transcript.

"I'll talk anywhere": Katharine Hayhoe, "How to Talk About Climate Change So People Will Listen," Chatelaine, April 18, 2019, https://www .chatelaine.com/living/how-to-talk-about-climate-change/.

evangelical beliefs intersect: Sharareh Drury, "Late Night Hosts Unite to Spotlight Climate Change," *Hollywood Reporter*, September 22, 2021, https://www.hollywoodreporter.com/tv/tv-news/late-night-hosts -spotlight-climate-change-1235019060/.

"matters of the heart": Dan Zak, "One of America's Top Climate Scientists Is an Evangelical Christian. She's on a Mission to Persuade Skeptics," *Washington Post*, July 15, 2019, https://www.washington post.com/lifestyle/style/one-of-americas-top-climate-scientists-is -an-evangelical-christian-shes-on-a-mission-to-convert-skeptics /2019/07/12/9018094c-8d2a-11e9-adf3-f70f78c156e8_story.html.

"Katharine Hayhoe is a national treasure": Jon Schwartz, "Katharine Hayhoe, a Climate Explainer Who Stays Above the Storm," *New York Times*, October 10, 2016, https://www.nytimes.com/2016/10/11 /science/katharine-hayhoe-climate-change-science.html.

One of the 100 Most Influential: Don Cheadle, "Katharine Hayhoe: An Environmental Evangelist," *Time*, April 23, 2014, https://time.com /collection-post/70881/katharine-hayhoe-2014-time-100/.

"changed their mind": Hayhoe, "Honours I've Received," http://www .katharinehayhoe.com/biography/.

"isn't something we notice directly": Katharine Hayhoe, "A Climate for All of Us," The Nature Conservancy, November 11, 2021, https://www .nature.org/en-us/magazine/magazine-articles/climate-justice -hayhoe/.

"absolutely not fair": Dan Falk, "Interview: Katharine Hayhoe on How to Talk About Climate Change," *Undark*, November 5, 2021, https:// undark.org/2021/11/05/katharine-hayhoe-interview/.

"danger from the mafia": Hayhoe, *Saving Us*, 22.

"someone who takes the Bible seriously": Gina Ciliberto, "Despite Hate from Evangelicals, Katharine Hayhoe Sees Climate Hope," *Sojourners*, April 20, 2021, https://sojo.net/articles/despite-hate-evangelicals -katharine-hayhoe-sees-climate-hope.

"Wow, you can do that?": Marcia Bosscher, "Taking your Baby with You: An Interview with Katharine Hayhoe," The Well, Intervarsity, March 31, 2016, https://thewell.intervarsity.org/voices/taking-your -baby-you-interview-katharine-hayhoe.

"shut me up": Katharine Hayhoe, Instagram, September 22, 2021, https:// www.instagram.com/p/CUFlEnJrwx0/.

"I love my son": Katharine Hayhoe, Instagram, September 17, 2021, https:// www.instagram.com/p/CT5ou_6MkBT/.

"organizations are divesting": Katharine Hayhoe, "The Real Science of Climate Change," interview by Peter McCormack, February 17, 2020, *Defiance* (podcast), episode 29, https://static1.squarespace.com/static/5d177 c95be7bcb000149b1f8/t/5e69b507cf22dd4b193e9a75/1583985933641 /DEF029+-+Prof.+Katharine+Hayhoe+Transcription.pdf.

Chapter 7: Jacquelyn Gill

"jump into a time machine": *Lost Beasts of the Ice Age*, episode 1, February 5, 2019, https://www.discovery.com/shows/lost-beasts-of-the-ice -age/episodes/lost-beasts-of-the-ice-age; Wilcox Welness & Fitness, "'Training Saved My Life'—Jacquelyn Gill," client interview, May 21, 2019, https://www.wilcoxwellnessfitness.com/newsletter—blog /training-saved-my-life-jacquelyn-gill.

"We actually call them mummies": All quotes from original author interview with Jacquelyn Gill on March 30, 2021, unless otherwise noted here.

"Serengeti of the ice age"': Beth Staples, "Mereghetti Analyzes 'Time Capsules' from Last Ice Age," UMaine News, October 26, 2021, https://umaine .edu/news/blog/2021/10/26/mereghetti-analyzes-time-capsules -from-last-ice-age/.

soil, gravel, and sand: "Permaforst," National Geographic (website), https:// www.nationalgeographic.org/encyclopedia/permafrost/.

craters ripping: Brian Kahn, "Everything Is Extremely Normal and Totally Fine," Gizmodo, September 1, 2020, https://gizmodo.com/every thing-is-extremely-normal-and-totally-fine-1844909673.

will not spare Siberia: Isaac Schultz, "Ground Temperatures Hit 118 Degrees in the Arctic Circle," June 22, 2021, https://gizmodo.com/ground -temperatures-hit-118-degrees-in-the-arctic-circl-1847144505.

permafrost is thawing: Isabelle Khurshudyan, Andrew Freedman and Brady Dennis, "Rapid Arctic Meltdown in Siberia Alarms Scientists," *Washington Post*, July 3, 2020, https://www.washingtonpost.com /climate-environment/rapid-arctic-meltdown-in-siberia-alarms -scientists/2020/07/03/4c1bd6a6-bbaa-11ea-bdaf-a129f921026f_story .html.

"phalanx of badassery": Dr. Jacquelyn Gill, Twitter post, May 24, 2019, https://twitter.com/JacquelynGill/status/1131919005797765130.

"There's nothing that doesn't already have our fingerprint on it": All quotes within "Trailblazer: Beth Shapiro" sidebar from original author interview with Beth Shapiro on October 18, 2021.

Chapter 8: Brigitte Baptiste

"I like strong coffee!": All quotes from original author interview with Brigitte Baptiste on September 1, 2021, unless otherwise noted here.

"if Earth's biodiversity": Chris Bell, "Here's Why Colombia Is One of the Most Biodiverse Countries on Earth," Culture Trip, September 2, 2021, https://theculturetrip.com/south-america/colombia/articles/heres-why-colombia-is-one-of-the-most-biodiverse-countries-on-earth/.

"her legacy has impacted biodiversity conservation": Ana María Enciso, "Three Extraordinary Transgender Latinas You Should Know," *BELatina*, June 28, 202, https://belatina.com/three-extraordinary-transgender-latinas/.

"nothing queerer than nature": Brigitte Baptiste, "Nothing More Queer than Nature," TEDx Talks, uploaded December 15, 2018, https://www.ted.com/talks/brigitte_baptiste_nada_mas_queer_que_la_naturaleza/transcript?language=en.

"We love you, Sarah!": "HRC's Sarah McBride addresses the 2016 Democratic National Convention," posted by Human Rights Commission, YouTube video, July 29, 2016, https://youtu.be/watch?v=EA9PeYZ7rrI.

Obama's keynote: Josh Paunil, "From 'Unwavering Ache' to Advocacy: Sarah McBride's Journey Breaking Barriers as a Transgender Woman," *Lily*, January 18, 2018, https://www.thelily.com/from-unwavering-ache-to-advocacy-sarah-mcbrides-journey-breaking-barriers-as-a-transgender-woman/.

"I hope tonight": Gwen Aviles, "Transgender Candidates Make Election History," *Harpers Bazaar*, November 4, 2020, https://www.harpersbazaar.com/culture/politics/a34567467/election-2020-trans-winners/.

it's all about funding: Samantha Riedel, "Vermont's First Trans State Representative Is Fighting for Her Community," Them, September 4, 2020, 4, 2020, https://www.them.us/story/trans-state-representative-taylor-small-interview.

"We are stronger than we know": Anne Branigin, "Andrea Jenkins Is the Nation's First Openly Trans City Council President. Here's Her Plan for Minneapolis," *Lily*, January 12, 2022, https://www.thelily.com/andrea-jenkins-is-the-nations-first-openly-trans-city-council-president-heres-her-plan-for-minneapolis/.

Chapter 9: Jeanette Davis

"I thought, If you love science, then you go to medical school": All quotes from original author interview with Jeanette Davis on June 2, 2021, unless otherwise noted here.

"You're too ambitious": @dr_ocean24, "Gender & Race Gap in STEM," Instagram, December 1, 2021, https://www.instagram.com/p/CW8c6ueluBU/.

birdwatching confrontation: Sarah Maslin Nir, "The Bird Watcher, That Incident and His Feelings on the Woman's Fate," *New York Times*, May 27, 2020, https://www.nytimes.com/2020/05/27/nyregion/amy -cooper-christian-central-park-video.html.

"to be seen and take up space": School of Environmental and Forest Sciences, "MISS & BWEEMS—Supporting Minorities in Ecological Sciences," student blog, University of Washington College of the Environment, February 23, 2022, https://sefs.uw.edu/students/student-blog-post /miss-minorities-in-shark-sciences/.

"The cover had a close-up picture of a shark": All quotes within "Trailblazer: Carlee Jackson" sidebar from original author interview with Carlee Jackson on December 11, 2021, unless otherwise noted here.

"None of us truly understood": "Nurse Shark," National Geographic (website), https://www.nationalgeographic.com/animals/fish/facts/nurse-shark.

Thanks to these four scientists: Ocean Conservancy, "Representation Matters: Welcome to Minorities in Shark Sciences," *Ocean Currents* (blog), August 12, 2020, https://oceanconservancy.org/blog/2020/08/12 /representation-matters-welcome-minorities-shark-sciences/.

"They're listed as endangered in the United States": All quotes within "Trailblazer: Jasmin Graham" sidebar from original author interview with Jasmin Graham on December 10, 2021, unless otherwise noted here.

thrive in salty water: Florida Department of Environmental Protection, "Florida's Mangroves" (web page), last modified May 23, 2022, https://floridadep.gov/rcp/rcp/content/floridas-mangroves.

mangrove forests are cleared: "The Importance of Mangroves," The Nature Conservancy, May 4, 2020, https://www.nature.org/en-us/about-us /where-we-work/united-states/florida/stories-in-florida/why -mangroves-important/.

"next generation of conservation leaders": Ryan Zlatanova, "Meet Jasmin Graham, WWF's 2021 Conservation Leadership Award Winner," World Wildlife Fund, November 17, 2021, https://www.worldwildlife.org /stories/meet-jasmin-graham-wwf-s-2021-conservation-leadership -award-winner.

"Water has always been a safe space for me": All quotes within "Trailblazer: Leslie Townsell" sidebar from original author interview with Leslie Townsell on December 12, 2021.

visibility of Black marine scientists: See https://www.tiaramoore.com/.

Chapter 10: Nikki Roach

"My fear is anxiety itself": All quotes from original author interview with Nikki Roach on August 23, 2021, unless otherwise noted here.

"yell leaders": Wikipedia, s.v. "Texas A&M University," https://en.wikipedia. org/wiki/Texas_A%26M_University.

Colombian coffee farmers: Richard Schiffman, "Colombian Coffee Farmers Are Paying the Price for Climate Change," Grist July 20, 2019, https:// grist.org/article/colombian-coffee-farmers-are-paying-the-price -for-climate-change/.

0.3 degrees: Richard Schiffman, "As Climate Changes, Colombia's Small Coffee Farmers Pay the Price," Yale Environment 360, July 11, 2019, https://e360.yale.edu/features/as-climate-changes-colombias-small -coffee-farmers-pay-the-price.

$2 a day: Amanda Panella, "An Assessment of Poverty in Columbia," https:// borgenproject.org/assessment-poverty-in-colombia, The Borgen Project, August 15, 2016.

agricultural breadwinner: Schiffmann, "Colombian Coffee."

wildlife or land trust: "What Does a Conservation Biologist Do?," Unity College (website), https://unity.edu/careers/conservation-biologist.

Chapter 11: Amy Cardinal Christianson

"For me, fire was a part of life": All quotes from original author interview with Amy Cardinal Christianson on April 27, 2021, unless otherwise noted here.

colonizers squashed: Lisa Szabo, "Five Things I've Learned About Good Fire," *New Trail*, September 23, 2021, https://www.ualberta.ca/newtrai l/people/five-things-ive-learned-about-good-fire.html.

"Don't fear fire": *YourForest* (podcast), episode 64, "Good Fire with Amy Cardinal Christianson," June 2019, https://open.spotify.com /episode/72dcBw4ggDsCgU1ilgNqFf.

"Fire season is interminable here": All quotes within "How Good Fire Can Help Our Forests" sidebar from original author interview with Alejandra Borunda on March 16, 2022.

fire is a natural part: Alejandra Borunda, "More 'Good Fire' Could Help California Control Future Catastrophes," *National Geographic*, July 27, 2021, https://www.nationalgeographic.com/environment/article /more-good-fire-could-help-california-control-future-catastrophes.

Prescribed burns . . . are effective: To learn more about prescribed burns, visit https://www.nps.gov/articles/what-is-a-prescribed-fire.htm.

"Do you know those sad stories": I attended this workshop with IJNR in which Debra spoke on November 17, 2021: http://www.ijnr.org/er _indigenous.

"My beat is Indians": Debra Utacia Krol, contributor profile, *Arizona Republic*, https://www.azcentral.com/staff/2684011001/debra-utacia -krol/.

"What Muir didn't recognize": Debra Utacia Krol, "'Living with Fire' May Lead to Less Destructive Wildfires, Say Indigenous Land Stewards," *Arizona Republic*, August 27, 2020, https://www.azcentral.com/story /news/local/arizona-wildfires/2020/08/27/indigenous-leaders-say -people-need-balance-land-wildfire/5624268002/.

"I would like to see a bit more": All quotes within "Trailblazer: Debra Utacia Krol" sidebar from original author interview with Debra Utacia Krol on November 11, 2021, unless otherwise noted here.

"At least two tribes": Debra Utacia Krol, "New Climate Report Wasn't Surprising to Indigenous Peoples, Who See Change up Close," *Arizona Republic*, August 20, 2021, https://www.azcentral.com/story/news /local/arizona/2021/08/20/un-climate-change-report-no-surprise -indigenous-peoples/8109461002/.

TEK means: US Fish & Wildlife Service, "Traditional Ecological Knowledge Fact Sheet," February 1, 2011, https://www.fws.gov/nativeamerican /pdf/tek-fact-sheet.pdf; Debra Utacia Krol, "Covering Indigenous Communities with Respect and Sensitivity," The Open Notebook, June 18, 2019, https://www.theopennotebook.com/2019/06/18 /covering-indigenous-communities-with-respect-and-sensitivity/.

Chapter 12: Anna Jane Joyner

"which I don't advise doing": All quotes from original author interview with Anna Jane Joyner on April 19, 2021, unless otherwise noted here.

"The stars were insane": Anna Jane, "The Uses of Sorrow," November 2021, *No Place like Home* (podcast), season 4, episode 3 https://open.spotify .com/episode/0DwLpHmmNfvN8R6CN5Iz1o.

"ever lucky enough": Eddie Widder, "Glowing in the Dark," Nova Science Now, PBS, accessed August 24, 2022, https://www.pbs.org/wgbh /nova/sciencenow/0305/04-glow-nf.html.

Bioluminescence is when: "Bioluminescence," National Geographic (website), https://www.nationalgeographic.org/encyclopedia/bioluminescence/.

creatures in the ocean: National Ocean and Atmospheric Administration, "Meet Edith A. Widder," Ocean Exploration, accessed on August 24, 2022   https://oceanexplorer.noaa.gov/edu/oceanage/04widder /welcome.html.

"That suit was not a comfortable ride!": From a PDF on Edie's website, accessed August 25, 2022, https://static.squarespace.com/static /529fa75be4b0aa09f5b7c01f/52a20fc5e4b0a31c291a8c80/52a20fc5e4b0a-31c291a8c93/1265746201183/Edie%20Widder%20Imagine%20Note.pdf.

"thrilling blend of hard science": Robert Moor, "The Wonders That Live at the Very Bottom of the Sea," *New York Times Book Review*, August 20, 2021, https://www.nytimes.com/2021/08/20/books/review /below-edge-darkness-edith-widder-brilliant-abyss-helen-scales-deep-ocean.html.

"thrown me out": Jane, "Uses of Sorrow."

"literally went from hell to heaven": Jane, "Uses of Sorrow."

"moral struggle": Judith A. Ross, "Years of Living Dangerously—Why We Can't Give Up," the green divas (website), https://thegreendivas .com/2014/05/17/years-of-living-dangerously-why-we-cant-give-up/.

father agreed to be filmed: *Years of Living Dangerously*, episode 4, "Ice & Brimstone," May 4, 2014.

"open as I possibly could": Scott Shigeoka, "Undaunted," *Grist*, December 23, 2019, https://grist.org/climate/the-climate-activist-who-hasnt-given -up-on-mainstream-america/.

"stewardship of creation": Anna Jane, "An Open Letter to My Daddy Who Doesn't Accept Climate Change," HuffPost, July 2, 2014, https://www .huffpost.com/entry/an-open-letter-to-my-dadd_b_5254040.

"in time for war": Jason Lemon, "Evangelical Pastor Urges Christians to 'Mobilize' to Fight Civil War Against Left-Wing Activists," Newsweek, September 14, 2020, https://www.newsweek.com/evangelical -pastor-urges-christians-mobilize-fight-civil-war-against-left-wing -activists-1531827.

"Sally was a really bad storm": Jane, "Uses of Sorrow."

"Climate change is making it more likely": Veronica Penney, "What We Know About Climate Change and Hurricanes," *New York Times*,

August 29, 2021, https://www.nytimes.com/2021/08/29/climate
/climate-change-hurricanes.html.

"stepping on the accelerator": Sarah Kaplan, "How Climate Change Helped
Make Hurricane Ida One of Louisiana's Worst," *Washington Post*,
August 30, 2021, https://www.washingtonpost.com/climate-environ
ment/2021/08/29/how-climate-change-helped-make-hurricane-ida
-one-louisianas-worst/.

end of the last ice age: Kaplan, "Hurricane Ida."

"a state of high anxiety and stress": Mary Anne Hitt and Anna Jane Joyner, "S4
Ep 3 | The Uses of Sorrow: Anna Jane," November 17, 2021, *No Place
Like Home* podcast, https://podcasts.apple.com/us/podcast/s4-ep-3
-the-uses-of-sorrow-anna-jane/id1158028749?i=1000542227288.

surveyed 10,000: Tosin Thompson, "Young People's Climate Anxiety
Revealed in Landmark Survey," September 22, 2022, https://www
.nature.com/articles/d41586-021-02582-8.

"driving force": Joyner, "Uses of Sorrow."

Chapter 13: Jennifer Uchendu

"We really want to see rapid and urgent action": All quotes from original
author interview with Jennifer Uchendu on May 27, 2021, unless
otherwise noted here.

highest deforestation rates: See "Nigeria," "National Geographic Kids,"
https://kids.nationalgeographic.com/geography/countries/article
/nigeria; Wikipedia, s.v. "Deforestation in Nigeria," last modified July 21, 2022, https://en.wikipedia.org/wiki/Deforestation_in
_Nigeria.

rosewood logs: Rachel Nuwer, "Illegal Logging Has Become More Violent than
Ever," *National Geographic*, February 3, 2016, https://www.national
geographic.com/animals/article/160202-Illegal-loggers-murders
-violence-defending-land; "Rosewood Robbery: A Case for Thailand to List Rosewood on CITES," report, Environmental Investigation Agency, February 16, 2012, https://eia-international.org/wp
-content/uploads/Rosewood-Robbery.pdf; Matthew T. Page, "The
Intersection of China's Commercial Interests and Nigeria's Conflict
Landscape," special report, US Institute of Peace, September 1, 2018,
http://www.jstor.com/stable/resrep20240.

"stop deforestation by 2030": Jennifer Uchendu, "Activism at COP 26 Summit
+ Nigeria & Climate Change," November 7, 2021, YouTube video,
https://youtu.be/watch?v=rNTjtHyVAPE.

"Young people are frightened": Nimi Princewill, "Africa's Most Populous City Is Battling Floods and Rising Seas. It May Soon Be Unlivable, Experts Warn," CNN, August 2, 2021, https://edition.cnn.com/2021/08/01/africa/lagos-sinking-floods-climate-change-intl-cmd/index.html.

"vulnerable and so marginalized": Isobel Whitcomb, "Is It Time to Abandon the Term 'Climate Anxiety'?," *Yes!*, August 31, 2021, https://www.yesmagazine.org/environment/2021/08/31/climate-anxiety-mental-health.

"gloomy reflections": Jennifer, Uchendu, "Eco-anxiety and the Politics of Hope: A Reflective Opportunity to Build Resilience," Institute of Development Studies, February 6, 2020, https://alumni.ids.ac.uk/news/blogs-perspectives-provocations-initiatives/515/515-Eco-anxiety-and-the-politics-of-hope-a-reflective-opportunity-to-build-resilience.

"our forests, freshwater": Jennifer Uchendu, "Climate Change Conversation: Jennifer Reminds Us That We Have a Crisis on Our Hands & We Need to Act NOW," interview by BellaNaija, October 18, 2019, https://www.bellanaija.com/2019/10/bn-climate-change-jennifer-uchendu/.

"all hands on deck": Sour, "How to Engage Millennials in Sustainable Community Development, ft. Jennifer Uchendu," December 21, 2020, *What's Wrong With* podcast, https://www.sour.studio/podcast/how-to-engage-millennials-in-sustainable-community-development-ft-jennifer-uchendu.

"government inaction": Tosin Thompson, "Young People's Climate Anxiety Revealed in Landmark Survey," *Nature*, September 22, 2021, https://www.nature.com/articles/d41586-021-02582-8.

"women play critical roles": Jennifer Uchendu, "For the Climate's Sake, Empower African Women," D+C Development and Cooperation, March 10, 2021, https://www.dandc.eu/en/article/global-heating-affects-poor-women-developing-countries-particularly-hard.

"I don't just tell stories": Ruth Green, "Ugochi Anyaka Oluigbo: A Race against Time," Women in Journalism, accessed on August 24, 2022, https://womeninjournalism.co.uk/profile-of-ugochi-anyaka-oluigbo-a-race-against-time-by-ruth-green.

"companies like Royal Dutch Shell" through *"It won't heal the damage"*: Westervelt, "We Don't Have the Power to Fight It," transcript, *Scene on Radio* (podcast), season 5, episode 6, http://www.sceneonradio.org/wp-content/uploads/2021/11/S5E6_transcript1_FINAL.pdf.

"He planted that seed early": All quotes within "Trailblazer: Ugochi Any-aka-Oluigbo" sidebar from original author interview with Ugochi Anyaka-Oluigbo on December 10, 2021, unless otherwise noted here.

Chapter 14: Tessa Khan

"These options definitely exist": All quotes from original author interview with Tessa Khan on March 3, 2021, unless otherwise noted here.

"fossil fuel racism": Tim Donaghy and Charlie Jiang, *Fossil Fuel Racism: How Phasing Out Oil, Gas, and Coal Can Protect Communities* (Washington: Greenpeace, 2021), https://www.greenpeace.org/usa/reports/fossil-fuel-racism/.

"global toll of premature deaths": Clara Chaisson, "Fossil Fuel Air Pollution Kills One in Five People," NRDC, February 19, 2021, https://www.nrdc.org/stories/fossil-fuel-air-pollution-kills-one-five-people.

"oil giants that have helped drive": Tessa Kahn, "Shell's Historic Loss in The Hague Is a Turning Point in the Fight Against Big Oil," *Guardian*, June 1, 2021, https://www.theguardian.com/commentisfree/2021/jun/01/shell-historic-loss-hague-fight-big-oil.

170 million barrels of oil: "Cambo Oil Field Development off Shetland to Be Paused," BBC, December 10, 2021, https://www.bbc.com/news/uk-scotland-59608521.

"We're here to stop them": #StopCambo (website), archived December 10, 2021, https://web.archive.org/web/20211210175057/https://www.stopcambo.org.uk/.

"UN and International Energy Agency agree": Tessa Kahn, "Cambo Has Been Halted—But Britain's Love Affair with Oil and Gas Isn't Over," Novara Media, December 10, 2021, https://novaramedia.com/2021/12/10/cambo-has-been-halted-but-britains-love-affair-with-oil-and-gas-isnt-over/.

"We need Cambo": Fiona Harvey, "Shell Pulls Out of Cambo Oilfield Project," *Guardian*, December 2, 2021, https://www.theguardian.com/environment/2021/dec/02/shell-pulls-out-of-cambo-oilfield-project; Abbi Garton-Crosbie, "Stop Cambo Architect Tessa Khan on the 'Chaotic Collapse' of the Oil Industry," *National*, December 10, 2021, https://www.thenational.scot/news/19777389.stop-cambo-architect-tessa-khan-chaotic-collapse-oil-industry/; @stopcambo, Instagram, December 12, 2021, https://www.instagram.com/p/CXZWXacFspc/.

"opening new oil": Kahn, "Cambo Has Been Halted."

"Water is an essential resource": All quotes within "Trailblazer: Newsha Ajami" sidebar from original author interview with Newsha Ajami on October 19, 2022, unless otherwise noted here.

"every drop of water properly": Todd Woody, "One of California's Wealthiest Counties Could Run Out of Water," Bloomberg, October 25, 2021, https:// www.bloomberg.com/news/features/2021-10-22/will-this-wealthy -california-town-run-out-of-water; Paul Rogers, "California Drought: Wasting Water? You Could Be Hit with a $500 Fine," *Mercury News*, December 6, 2021, https://www.mercurynews.com/2021/12/06 /california-drought-waste-water-you-could-be-hit-with-a-500-fine/; Katrina Swartz, "12 Important Things to Know About California's Drought," KQED, September 3, 2021, https://www.kqed.org/news /11887435/12-important-things-to-know-about-californias-drought.

Chapter 15: Anushka Saia Bhaskar

"We took a little rope that was one square meter": All quotes from original author interview with Anushka Saia Bhaskar on May 19, 2021, unless otherwise noted here.

"Algalita has changed my life": "Meet Algalita's Chief Youth Officer— Anushka Bhaskar," October 1, 2018, https://algalita.org/meet -algalitas-chief-youth-office-anushka-bhaskar/.

Great Pacific Garbage Patch: See https://plasticparadisemovie.com/.

world's biggest plastic polluter: Damian Carrington, "'Deluge of Plastic Waste': US Is World's Biggest Plastic Polluter," *Guardian* December 7, 2021, https://www.theguardian.com/environment/2021/dec/01 /deluge-of-plastic-waste-us-is-worlds-biggest-plastic-polluter.

between four and a half and six pounds: "U.S. Should Create National Strategy by End of 2022 to Reduce Its Increasing Contribution to Global Ocean Plastic Waste, Says New Report," National Academies, December 1, 2021 https://www.nationalacademies.org/news/2021/12/u-s-should -create-national-strategy-by-end-of-2022-to-reduce-its-increasing -contribution-to-global-ocean-plastic-waste-says-new-report.

still burn plastic: Ata Owaji Victor, "Beyond Reduce, Reuse, Recycle: How Beauty Can Navigate the Climate Crisis Post-COP26," *Elle*, December 3, 2021, https://www.elle.com/uk/beauty/a38409988/beauty-climate -crisis-post-cop26/.

plastic consumption increased: "Making Waves with Nextwave Plastics," Lonely Whale, March 25, 2021, https://www.lonelywhale.org/nextwave -plastics-2020-report.

moratorium on new plastic-producing: "To Tackle Plastic Pollution, We Need Big, Systemic Change," Sierra Club, https://www.sierraclub .org/do-your-part-and-help-end-single-use-plastic-pollution-2.

single-use plastics: See http://www.byebyeplasticbags.org.

marched from Paradise: *Generation on Fire* (documentary), Sunrise Movement, uploaded September 24, 2021, https://www.youtube.com /watch?v=Ocu2WwMMha8.

"outraged and hopeless": Lola Guthrie, "California Teen: I'm Marching 266 Miles, from Paradise to San Francisco, for Climate Justice," *Sacramento Bee*, June 7, 2021, https://www.sacbee.com/opinion/op-ed /article251903963.html.

support a Civilian Climate Corps: I interviewed Lola for an essay I wrote here: https://institute.dmns.org/perspectives/posts/youth-to-grown-ups -when-will-you-finally-do-something/.

CCC would also invest back into communities: Tik Root, "9 Questions About the Civilian Climate Corps, Answered," *Washington Post*, September 16, 2021, https://www.washingtonpost.com/climate -solutions/2021/09/16/civilian-climate-corps-explained/.

"fossil fuel executives have subverted": Personal email from Park Guthrie, October 22, 2021.

water down his commitments: Davis Smith, "'Tired of Broken Promises': Climate Activists Launch Hunger Strike Outside White House," *Guardian*, October 20 2021, https://www.theguardian.com/environment /2021/oct/20/sunrise-movement-climate-activists-hunger-strike.

"Ema is understandably daunted": Guthrie email, October 22, 2021.

"We turned out": Kerry Benefield, "Young Santa Rosa Climate Activist Participates in Hunger Strike Outside White House," *Press Democrat*, October 28, 2021 https://www.pressdemocrat.com/article/news /santa-rosa-student-leader-in-climate-hunger-strike-outside-white -house/.

"thrilled to be part": "Harvard, Earth Friendly Products Host Environmental Summit," Sal DiDomenico (official website), October 9, 2019, https://www.senatordidomenico.com/newsroom/2020/9/21 /harvard-earth-friendly-products-host-environmental-summit.

coined the term intersectional environmentalism: See https://www.inter sectionalenvironmentalist.com/.

"exacerbating environmental and health inequity": Anushka Bhaskar, "The Climate Crisis Is a Health Crisis," *Ecosia* (blog), October 20, 2020, https://blog.ecosia.org/climate-crisis-health-crisis/.

Notes

"We really need to change the system": See https://www.climatercommunities .org/.

"I see a lot of disparities": All quotes within "Trailblazer: Violet Wulf-Saena" sidebar from original author interview with Violet Wulf-Saena on October 15, 2021, unless otherwise noted here.

"commitment to policies with funding": Ezra David Romero, "A Diverse City Vulnerable to Flooding Rallies for Protection," April 23, 2021, *All Things Considered* (radio show), NPR, https://www.npr .org/2021/04/23/990281500/climate-migrants-battle-flooding-again.